P9-CAJ-652

CHEF WOLFE'S
NEW
AMERICAN
TURKEY
COOKERY

★ ★ ★ ★ ★ ★ ★ ★ ★ ★ ★ ★ ★

KEN WOLFE · OLGA BIER

CHEF WOLFE'S *NEW* AMERICAN TURKEY COOKERY

★ ★ ★ ★ ★ ★ ★ ★ ★ ★ ★ ★ ★ ★

KEN WOLFE • OLGA BIER

illustrations by Amy Pertschuk

photographs by Marshall Berman

*edited and recipes tested
by Maggie Blyth Klein*

A STEP-BY-STEP MASTER CLASS
WITH TECHNIQUES, THEORIES,
AND RECIPES

ARIS BOOKS

Addison-Wesley Publishing Company, Inc.
Reading, Massachusetts Menlo Park, California New York
Don Mills, Ontario Wokingham, England Amsterdam Bonn
Sydney Singapore Tokyo Madrid San Juan

★ ★

Copyright © 1984 by Ken Wolfe and Olga Bier
Turkey Day © 1984 by Charles Perry

All rights reserved. No part of this publication may be reproduced, stored in a retrieval
system, or transmitted, in any form or by any means, electronic, mechanical, photocopying,
recording, or otherwise, without the prior written permission of the publisher. Printed in
the United States of America. Printed simultaneously in Canada.

ISBN 0-201-11803-3, pbk.
(Previously published by Harris Publishing Co.,
ISBN 0-943186-17-X, pbk.)

Sharon Smith Design
Typesetting by Design & Type

Produced by L. John Harris

Aris Books Editorial Office and Test Kitchen
1621 Fifth Street
Berkeley, California 94710

Manufactured in the United States of America
First Addison-Wesley printing, March 1989
ABCDEFGHIJ-VB-89

For Janet and Harry, with love

Contents

Foreword

I had at least fifteen old-fashioned, bread-stuffed, dry-breasted Thanksgiving turkeys to my so-called credit before something happened to put an end to all that.

Just before Thanksgiving four years ago a friend brought me a clipping from the food section of our local newspaper. The article, written by Olga Bier, described a new way to roast the Thanksgiving turkey, a way devised by Chef Ken Wolfe. In the article, Wolfe gave directions for dismantling the cherished family bird, cooking it a couple of hours, and serving it with stuffing made in its own pan and flavored with skin and parts from the turkey or with fat from another source altogether. I thought the idea fanatical. If my friend hadn't dared me (there may even have been money involved), Chef Wolfe's method of cooking a turkey would never have been tried at the Kleins' house, rest assured. I was too cowardly and too unimaginative to have veered from the traditional path.

But I had been dared. I followed the instructions to the letter. I had to admit that the finished reassembled bird was just as beautiful as ever, even though it rode a little low on the serving platter. My husband carved the roast in a minute and, best of all, the breast meat was the most moist I'd ever tasted. You could cut it with a fork. The dark meat was roasted to perfection. I had enough parts (the back, wing tips, and so on) to enable me to get a jump on making stock while the turkey roasted.

My friend called me the next day. She'd made her turkey the new way too, and reported the same superb results. We talked about it for a few days —you'd think we'd been in on the first moonwalk.

The following Thanksgiving a number of families with whom my husband and I are friends rented two adjoining vacation cottages for a country holiday. We planned a big mid-day bash; each household was to contribute a large turkey, vegetables, and desserts. I told the turkey cook at the other cottage she'd be missing a good bet if she left her turkey whole, in the fashion of the Dark Ages. She wasn't convinced. I got up Thanksgiving morning at 9:30, and brought our bird next door at noon, roasted to perfection. Sandy's bird was okay. The breast was a little Saharan, of course. Her gravy, I will admit, was as good as mine; we both had pan drippings to make it from. Her turkey was much more difficult to carve. And Sandy didn't look so swell, having been up since 5:30 a.m. I retained my usual sportsmanlike demeanor.

Over the next couple of years I kept

my ears and eyes open for mention of Chef Wolfe. I heard that a friend's daughter, with ambitions of becoming a professional cook, was elated to have gotten into one of his classes; an up-and-coming young *sous chef* told me of his reverence for Chef Wolfe; I was invited for an epicurean lunch at the college where he teaches.

Finally I met him at a gathering of food aficionados. Chef Wolfe proved to be as charming as he is inventive and masterful in the kitchen; he has a suave European manner with the right amount of cynical gleam in his eye.

Would I edit Chef Wolfe and Olga Bier's book, asked the publisher, John Harris? Do turkeys have feathers, I responded?

A note about Olga Bier. I hadn't met her until this project started. I knew she was an experienced writer and teacher of cooking (among other things), with a great admiration for Ken Wolfe, and a fine cook in her own right. I didn't know she'd prove to be an exuberant, excited, endlessly talented woman—a sensible perfectionist with a joy of life that is contagious.

—*Maggie Blyth Klein*

TURKEY DAY
by
Charles Perry

Did the Pilgrims eat turkey on the first Thanksgiving in 1620? Probably. *Probably.* According to their records some of the gentlemen went out and shot a lot of fowl, which probably included turkeys as well as ducks and geese, but the records simply don't specify.

If they did eat turkey, it was nothing exotic to them. The turkey may be native to the New World, but it had been raised in England since 1530. The first recipe for turkey to appear in an English cookbook was in Thomas Dawson's *The Good Huswife's Jewell,* published in 1586, and it is assumed that Queen Elizabeth I tasted turkey on at least one occasion in 1561. By the time of Gervase Markham's *The English Huswife*, published five years before the Pilgrims' voyage, turkey was apparently as common in England as chicken. It had proved so popular that it actually preempted the name of another bird, which we call the *guinea fowl* today. The guinea fowl had been introduced to England early in the 16th century as "turkey fowl" because it had originally been imported from African countries under Turkish rule. But the new bird from the New World, which the guinea fowl somewhat resembles, quickly made off with the name *turkey.*

If the Pilgrims ate turkey on the first Thanksgiving, they may have eaten it roasted but they are just as likely to have eaten it stewed. Their Thanksgiving was based on a Dutch holiday they had become familiar with during their sojourn in Holland, and the Dutch give thanks with a mixed stew they call *huitspot* or hodgepodge. Roasting is certainly not the exclusive way of cooking turkey in early cookbooks. The 1586 book gives a recipe for deboning a turkey and making it into a sort of sausage like the French *galantine*, which is still the most traditional way of serving turkey in New Orleans, where galantine has a long association with New Year's Day. Early English cookbooks also call for boiling turkey, then baking it in a lot of butter and making turkey pie, usually with a couple of chickens or rabbits to fill out the crust.

A large roasted fowl is indubitably festive, though, and roast turkey became a New England tradition early on. The colonists were probably already stuffing their turkeys with oysters in the 17th century. England was oyster-mad in the 17th and 18th centuries, even going so far as to stuff leg of lamb with oysters. As early as 1681 an English book recommends serving boiled turkey with a sauce of poached oysters, and the oyster was to accompany the turkey in many forms, such as in oyster sandwiches that garnished turkey stew.

Bread stuffings must have been around from the beginning too, even if cookbooks didn't deign to record such plain fare, and the colonists' heavy dependence on corn automatically inspired the cornbread stuffing. The other turkey stuffing most people know is chestnut, but this appears to be of German origins rather than Puritan.

How did Thanksgiving become Turkey Day? We have to remember that Thanksgiving was not a national holiday until the middle of the past century. It was locally celebrated in New England (with ham as often as with turkey), but not on a regular basis elsewhere. True, George Washington proclaimed a Day of Thanksgiving in 1784 and either the President or Congress often proclaimed Thanksgiving, at various dates in October and November, in the years that followed. It was scarcely ever celebrated in the South, however. When Governor Johns of Virginia proclaimed Thanksgiving Day in 1855, he found himself embroiled in controversy for trying to bring a Puritan holiday to his state. Nevertheless, two years later his successor

again proclaimed Thanksgiving in Virginia, and in 1858 eight Southern states were officially celebrating it.

The Civil War dampened the popularity of Thanksgiving in the South, but it ultimately adopted it as a national holiday. In 1864 Abraham Lincoln proclaimed it, naming the fourth Thursday in November as the date, with the clear intention of setting aside that date for Thanksgiving from then on: a uniform date, rather than the haphazard dates of the past, for a national holiday of first rank. The successors of the martyred president automatically followed his wishes. It fell in well with the mood of the late 19th century, when the United States was becoming a substantial member of the world community. Now that we had an official national harvest festival, it seemed inescapable that it should be celebrated with an indubitably American food. The mood is amusingly reflected in a cartoon that appeared in the souvenir program of the 1896 Thanksgiving Day Celebration of the American Club of London. It shows Mom and Pop Turkey (Mom in an 18th century cloth bonnet, Pop holding a flagpole) weeping for their son, who is enthroned in glory on a serving plate. "Dying for his country," says the merry caption.

The automatic association of Turkey with Thanksgiving might sound like a good thing for the early turkey farmers, but it seems actually to have been a disaster. From 1890, when the turkey dinner was standardized, to 1920, the number of turkeys raised annually plummeted from 11 million to 3.5 million at the same time that the human population had increased by 70 percent. The association had become *too* strong—turkey was thought of as being only for Thanksgiving, and, by association, for the other two holidays celebrated with a family dinner, Christmas and Easter. Until World War II, turkey was strictly special-occasion food and its sales reacted to economic fluctuations just like any semi-luxury item.

The turkey has spent the last 60-odd years recovering from the exclusive association with holidays. Turkey farmers still groan about the holiday curse, but even before widespread use of freezing made it convenient to offer turkey all year 'round, national consumption of turkey had gone from 1.8 pounds per capita in 1929 to 4.4 pounds in 1945. Now, with turkey franks and turkey hams and who knows what else, we can say the turkey is finally conquering Turkey Day.

Introduction

This is a cookbook of ideas and techniques—techniques developed by Chef Ken Wolfe over a period of 25 years utilizing the principles of thermodynamics and the correct application of heat to properly seasoned turkey. Just what does this mean to the cook of today? It means, quite simply, a tasty 22-pound turkey cooked to golden perfection in just a little more than 2 hours. There will have been no basting, no turning, no 6-hour roasting. All those time-consuming tasks commonly associated with turkey cooking are no longer necessary.

The only time-consuming task remaining is to master the simple techniques presented here for disassembling the traditional whole turkey into its major sections for roasting or other preparations.

The physics of heat With Ken Wolfe's approach, you will eliminate bones and waste and allow heat to penetrate the meat most effectively in the shortest time possible. The festive bird, roasted in its three major sections (two thigh-drumsticks and the breast), still can be presented on its traditional platter either to be carved at the table more easily than ever before, or to be boned and presliced in the kitchen. If you wish, you may select only the parts of the turkey you like and use those parts in any of the appropriate recipes presented in this book—all of which stress freshness of ingredients and simplicity of preparation.

Chef Wolfe's method is based on the principle that *it is not the weight of the turkey that determines the cooking time, but the thickness of the meat.* Applying this theory, Chef Wolfe has developed techniques of turkey preparation that result in juicy and tasty turkey and that liberate the cook. The recipes pre-

sented here are based on the understanding of the basic preparations. We suggest that the first three chapters of the book be read first so you will be familiar with the new methods before trying the recipes.

In addition to the happy holiday meal that turkey traditionally supplies, it is also a sound purchase for the consumer seeking nutritious, low-cost, high-quality protein. Turkey and its infinite varia-tions can now become part of the family's weekly menu with both financial and gastronomical dividends.

Although *Chef Wolfe's New American Turkey Cookery* emphasizes the value of understanding the culinary principles and techniques relevant to turkey cookery, no cookbook would be complete without delicious recipes. We have included dozens of recipes that use turkey in a variety of international dishes reflecting both modern adaptations of classic dishes as well as more contemporary fare.

About Chef Wolfe Classically trained as a chef in his native Austria, Chef Wolfe has cooked and lectured all over the world—from Europe to the Orient to Canada and finally to California. Before assuming directorship of the Culinary Arts Department of Contra Costa College, he worked at the Fairmont and Mark Hopkins hotels, and operated his own restaurant, in San Francisco. In great demand as an instructor and lecturer to chefs and dieticians all over the Bay Area, he created the program he now heads at the college, providing quality training for aspiring chefs and bakers.

At a time when interest in culinary arts is higher than ever before, Ken Wolfe's expertise, based on classical training and creative direction, marks him as one of the outstanding chef-educators of our time.

—Olga Bier

Some definitions...

al dente Firm to the bite.

bain-marie A double boiler. It can be improvised by setting a saucepan into another larger pot of hot water. The *bain-marie* will keep many dishes hot without danger of overcooking them or diminishing flavor.

blanch To dip briefly into boiling water to soften or set color.

butterfly To cut partway through meat, being careful not to sever it. The meat is "hinged" and opens like a book, creating a large, thin piece from a smaller, thick one.

caramelize To cook a substance containing sugar long enough to brown the sugar.

carcass The large bony cage that supports the breast and creates the framework of the body of the turkey. It consists of the ribs, keel, wishbone, and the vertebrae that comprise the back of the bird.

china cap A conical metal strainer, also called a *chinois*.

crop The pouchlike organ in the neck of the bird where preliminary digestion takes place. Its removal by meat processors creates the hollow of the neck—to be referred to in this book as the neck cavity. Giblets are often packed in this area (as well as in the larger body cavity) when the birds are prepared for market.

defat To remove fat by chilling and removing the layer of fat that rises to the top and solidifies.

deglaze Adding liquid, boiling, and scraping the cooked residue from a skillet or pan to incorporate and reduce.

dice To cut into approximately 1/2-inch cubes.

giblets The internal edible organs: stomach or gizzard, heart, and liver.

gravy The liquid prepared from a base of the roast's drippings.

julienne To cut into thin strips.

keel The large breast bone which separates the breast into two symmetrical parts.

mince To cut into the finest pieces possible.

mirepoix A mixture of equal parts onion, celery, and carrots, roughly cubed, to which a bay leaf or other herbs are sometimes added. The mixture is used to reinforce flavors.

recirculation or **setting time** The important resting period when the roasted meat is allowed to sit undisturbed after it is removed from the oven. This time allows the juices to recirculate throughout the flesh and to equalize the pressure and the heat, assuring a juicy turkey.

roux The thickening paste made from equal weights fat and flour used in sauces and gravies.

sauce Any liquid preparation made from stock, starch, fat, and a complementary flavor such as tomato, spices, wine, or cream. It is not based on the roast drippings.

sauté To cook briefly in a sauté pan (skillet) in a very small amount of fat.

scallopine, medallions, cutlets Terms that signify the size or shape

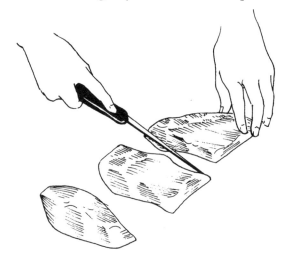

of the cut of meat. Scallopine are the smallest, three per serving; medallions, two per serving; and cutlets are the largest, one per serving.

shred To pull apart naturally on the fiber's grain into slender slivers.

simmer To cook just below the boiling point. At a boil, the surface will bubble and break. At a simmer, tiny bubbles gather around the rim of the pot but never actually break through the surface. If tested with a thermometer, the temperature should be 190° to 200° F.

zest The outermost layer of citrus fruit, which contains the flavor (oils) of the fruit. This is removed with a special zesting tool or it can be grated off.

About the ingredients...

butter All butter referred to in the following recipes is salted butter (four sticks to 1 pound; 4 ounces to one stick) unless otherwise specified. Unsalted butter has a higher fat content and lower water content and serves a specific purpose which is stated in the recipes in which it is used.

cilantro An herb, also known as Chinese parsley. Its leaves are from the coriander plant, a member of the parsley family.

coriander Refers to the dried seed or fruit of the plant. It has a lemony flavor.

eggs All eggs referred to in the following recipes are large, grade AA.

feta Originally a Greek cheese made of sheep's milk, now made in many countries. It is salty, dry, and white.

flour All flour referred to in the following recipes is all-purpose flour.

onions All onions referred to in the following recipes are the common yellow onion unless otherwise specified.

potatoes If potatoes are to be used in a salad, buy white or red (sometimes called *salad*) potatoes. Russets are for baking or mashing.

ricotta Italian unsalted dry cottage cheese.

tomatoes—peeling and deseeding To peel, plunge into boiling water for 15 to 20 seconds. Remove and immediately place in ice water to stop cooking. Cut out stem or core and lift off skins with a paring knife. To deseed, cut the tomato in half. Place half cut-side-up in the palm of your hand, turn your hand over, and gently squeeze while giving a snapping jerk with your wrist (over the sink or garbage container) so the seeds will drop out.

turkey It is important to remember that all the recipes in this book are based on the part or parts of a 22- to 24-pound turkey. Smaller turkey parts will require a possible adjustment of other ingredients as well as a change in temperature and cooking time.

CHAPTER ONE

BASIC
PREPARATION

★ ★

With new methods of breeding and nutrition, today's turkey has at least 25 percent more meat on its carcass than the turkey of the 1950's, bearing little resemblance to the wild bird that started the great American Thanksgiving tradition.

Whereas hens are generally marketed younger and therefore smaller, a tom or male turkey is your best buy—the larger the bird, the better. Even if you are planning a meal for a small number of people, a large tom is your wisest choice because of the higher ratio of meat to waste; you can freeze the

"Of course, any knife is good enough to cut your finger, but only a sharp knife is good enough to cut food." KW

As much as 95 percent of America's breeding stock is in California. Through scientific nutrition and genetic selection, turkey breeders bring a 22- to 24-pound tom turkey to market 18 weeks after hatching, with a high 60 percent yield of edible meat.

meat you do not cook for later use.

Birds that are even larger than 24 pounds can be found in the markets, but the wholesale price per pound of these birds is generally higher than for the slightly smaller birds. The largest turkeys are bought mainly by the food service trade and are served in dishes that call for chicken. The saving in time and labor in preparation for the amount of meat obtained is obvious and a major consideration of every food service operator.

GUIDELINES FOR SELECTION

Tenderizing injections, self-basting inserts, temperature gauges, and various other advertising inducements are unnecessary when you understand the correct way to cook turkey. The large tom has been bred for a plumper breast and legs. By sectioning, eliminating bones and waste, and equalizing the thickness of the meat, you can successfully prepare a dinner for two or a banquet for twelve without any of those promotional features.

After deciding on the occasion, the number of guests, and the particular dish or dishes you wish to prepare, it's off to the supermarket to select your bird. But because most turkeys are pre-packaged and frozen, it is almost impossible to judge their quality. As the cook, you must make a decision based on confidence in the packer, distributor, grocer, and the brands that you have used successfully before.

DEFROSTING

The trip home from the supermarket is a good start toward defrosting the frozen turkey. If you are going to cook it within 3 to 4 days, finish defrosting the turkey in the refrigerator. If you are going to cook it sooner than that, set it, covered, for up to 14 hours in a cool place that will not exceed 65° to 70° F. Then you must return it to the refrigerator until you are ready to wash it and proceed with sectioning and preparation.

If you purchase a "fresh" bird, it should be refrigerated and cooked or frozen immediately. The term *fresh* is actually a misnomer since it means only that the turkey is unfrozen. To use the term *fresh* is to imply that the frozen turkey is consequently "unfresh," which is not the case at all. Frozen birds, properly handled by reputable suppliers and markets and properly prepared by informed cooks, are as tasty, tender, and juicy as freshly killed birds.

UTENSILS AND EQUIPMENT

Proper tools are essential in boning and carving a turkey. You will need a high-quality boning knife with a 5- to 6-1/2-inch stainless steel flexible blade. It must be kept sharp with regular honing on a stone and frequent steeling with a sharpening steel. The old adage that you are more likely to cut yourself with a dull knife, which tends to slip, than with a sharp one holds quite true.

The cutting surface on which meat—especially poultry—is placed is extremely important. A board on which raw poultry has been cut provides a particularly desirable medium for the growth of salmonella bacteria. Porous surfaces such as wood must be scrupulously cleaned and sterilized with a 50 to 100 percent bleach solution that should be flooded over the board for at least 5 minutes. Then the board must be rinsed off and air dried to prevent any remaining bacteria from

Boning knife.

Boning knife.

Boning knife.

Boning knife.

Slicing knife.

Fluted carving knife.

multiplying and infecting other food placed on it.

The best cutting surface is of synthetic composition. A nonporous, synthetic board will not absorb the particles of flesh and blood that serve as media for bacterial growth and that transfer flavors—and you can put them in the dishwasher for cleaning and sterilization. Lightweight, nonporous boards come in many sizes that will serve a variety of your cooking needs.

Because effective carving is done with a sawing motion, the blade of your carving or slicing knife should be long—10 to 14 inches—thin, slightly flexible, and very sharp. It should not have a tapered end as does a chef's knife, but rather the blade should be an even width to its tip, which may be either pointed or rounded.

Carving board.

As with the boning knife, keep your carving knife sharp.

The carving board is simply a cutting board with a groove or trough around the edge to catch juices as they accumulate. Because cooked meat is not as conducive to the development of bacteria as is raw poultry, a wooden board is quite safe, provided it has been kept scrupulously clean.

STORAGE

After sectioning the turkey and deciding which parts you will use immediately, you can store the remaining parts for up to 2 days in properly packaged, airtight wrapping in a refrigerator that maintains a temperature range of 35° to 45° F.

If the parts are to be kept any longer than 2 days, they must be refrozen and held at 0° F in a properly functioning freezer. Brush the meat with oil before wrapping in plastic wrap for protection. Wrap the turkey parts for freezing as airtight as possible to prevent freezer burn, loss of flavor and texture, and absorption of other flavors.

An effective way to label and further insure an airtight wrap is to place a label with the name of the part and the date wrapped on top of the package and then wrap a second time. That gives a double wrap and prevents the loss of the label when you rearrange food in the freezer. Frozen parts should be used within 3 months for maximum flavor, so the date on the label is important.

Remember to make the package as flat as possible when you arrange the parts to be wrapped. The flatter it is, the quicker it will freeze —and the quicker it will thaw.

Bones for the stock can be labeled and frozen if you are not intending to make accompanying gravies and sauces for the parts you are cooking immediately. You may prefer, however, to start the stock pot at once, then strain and freeze the stock for later use.

THE BASIC CUTS

Removing the legs Pull the drumstick and thigh sideways away from the body. With a boning knife, slit

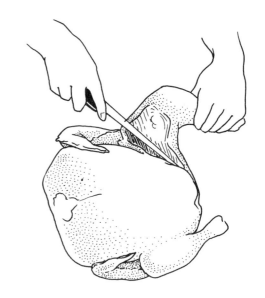

Pull drumstick and thigh away from body. With boning knife, slit skin to separate thigh from body.

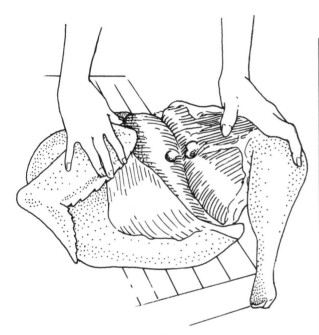

Slide turkey to edge of cutting board; hold breast down firmly with one hand; with other hand, press leg down over edge until hip joint snaps and head of thigh bone projects out of the socket.

the skin to separate the thigh from the body. Do not cut into the flesh.

Slide the turkey to the edge of the cutting board or table. Hold the breast down firmly with one hand, and with the other hand press the leg down over the edge until the hip joint snaps, projecting the head of the thigh bone up and out of the socket. Turn the turkey breast on its side with the disjointed leg on top and separate the leg more completely from the body.

Locate the small oval piece of meat that lies in the shallow basinlike depression of the lower back next to the backbone. This tender bit of flesh is called the *oyster*. With the tip of your boning knife, carefully cut around this choice bit of meat. Cut the leg free along the backbone, pulling the leg away gently as you cut.

Repeat the procedure to remove the other leg.

Removing the wings Pull the wing firmly away from the body and

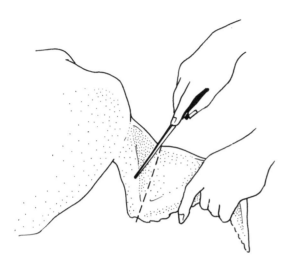

Pull wing firmly away from body and stretch it to its full length. Cut at second joint.

stretch it to its full length. Cut at the second joint, leaving the first section attached to the breast.

Cut the wing tip off at the last joint and set the two pieces from each wing (the tip and middle section) aside.

Removing the back Stand the turkey, with the legs removed, on its crop. Locate the last rib and cut along this rib diagonally through the body to the backbone. Repeat on the other side.

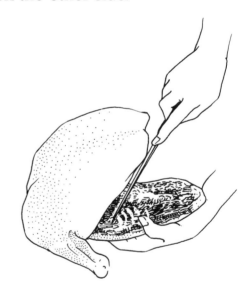

Stand turkey on crop. Locate last rib and cut along this rib diagonally through body to backbone. Repeat on other side. Snap and cut off lower back bone and skin.

Holding the tip of the turkey breast with one hand, pull the breast and back apart holding the tail end of the backbone with the other hand. It should break at the end of your diagonal cut (just above the oyster depression). Snap and cut off this piece of the lower back bone and skin, and set aside.

At this point, you should have the following parts from which we will be making the recipes in this book:

- the breast on the bone, cut in the new manner, with only the upper wing sections attached;
- two separate leg units each consisting of a thigh connected to a drumstick;
- the two center sections of each wing.

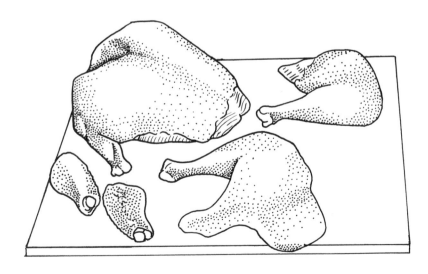

The two wing tips, the backbone of the carcass, and the neck, gizzard, heart, and skin trimmings will be used for making stock.

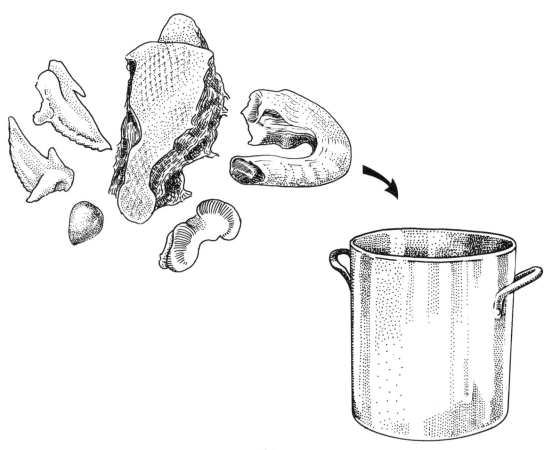

CHAPTER TWO

THE TRADITIONAL "WHOLE" TURKEY: MASTER RECIPE FOR THE TURKEY ROAST

★ ★

I f the ceremonial presentation of the whole turkey is part of your family's holiday tradition and if carving at the table is important to the occasion, you can roast a handsome "whole" turkey using the techniques of the new turkey cookery, with one major exception: it will take only 2-1/4 hours to cook! By disjointing and dividing the turkey according to the guidelines of Chapter 1, you can roast the breast, the turkey will look like Grandma's, but your family and guests will enjoy white meat that is more moist and tender than ever before. The dark meat will be juicy and rich, and the whole turkey will be easier to carve off the bone.

SEASONING

You may salt the skin of the breast and drumstick-thigh pieces if you

---

"Without salt we are not cooks." KW

---

bird (whole breast on the bone and two drumstick-thigh pieces), reassemble it on a platter, garnish it, and present it for carving at the head of the table. With the legs repositioned on each side of the base of wish, even though most of the salt will flow off the turkey with the melting fat of the skin. A light brushing with oil is needed, however, to help start the browning of the bird.

It is desirable to salt the uncovered flesh on the underside of the breast and legs. Place your hand inside the neck cavity and, with your fingers, gently loosen the skin away from the flesh. Stand the carcass crop-side up, pull the skin back, and salt the breast meat. Preferably, do this several hours before roasting for maximum penetration. Penetration is more effective when salt is applied to a moist surface. So, after you wash the meat, do not dry it; salt it while it is wet. The use of additional seasoning is optional—some cooks like to lay a bouquet of fresh herbs in the hollow under the breast—but, when properly salted, your turkey will require very little additional flavoring.

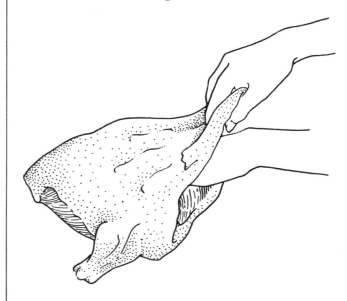

Salting the Breast and Thigh-Drumstick
⟶

Place hand inside crop; gently loosen skin.

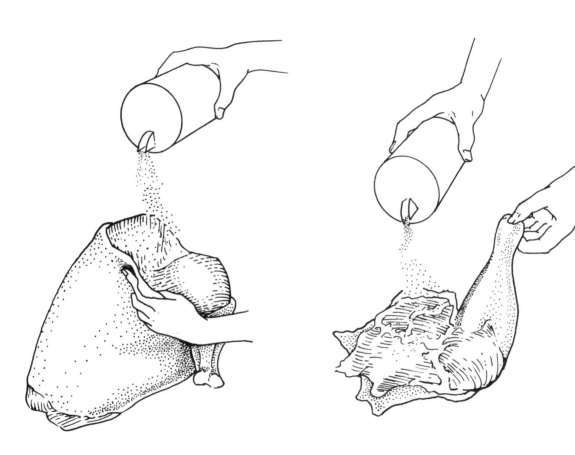

Stand carcass crop-side up, pull skin back, salt breast meat.

Salt underside of thigh-drumstick pieces.

THE ROASTING PROCESS

Roasting is cooking in the oven by dry heat (hot air) with a light addition of fat to commence browning. Roasts need no additional water. In fact, it is important to use a low-rimmed pan to assure that all developing steam be allowed to evaporate. (Never fear—enough juices will accumulate for delicious gravy. See Chapter 8—Gravy and Sauces.)

"How do traditions in cooking develop? Let me tell you a story. A young husband was seated at dinner and asked his wife why she cut off the ends of the ham. She replied, 'Because my mother always did it that way.' When he next saw his mother-in-law, he asked her why she cut off the ends of the ham. She answered, 'Because my mother always did it that way.' Fortunately, the old grandmother was still alive, so the next time he saw her he asked, 'Grandmother, why do you cut the ends off your ham?' 'So it will fit in my pan,' she replied." KW

Contrary to popular guidelines, the length of roasting time should not depend on the weight of the turkey. Roasting time depends on the size and type of roast, as well as the temperature of the oven and the temperature of the meat at the time it is put into the oven. It is the understanding of this principle that enables us to roast our turkey to perfection in a much shorter time than roasting a turkey without having disjointed it. (See chart p. 78.)

After you have disjointed the turkey (See Chapter 1), preheat your oven to 450° F—100° hotter than the temperature required for your roast.* The higher temperature will help compensate for the heat lost when you open the oven door and put in the cold turkey in its cold (oiled) pan.

Having cut away the heavy backbones and removed the two end sections of the wings (see p. 37), position the now-trimmed breast section in the oiled pan, neck-cavity side up. In that position it becomes self-basting because the fat in the skin will melt and flow over the breast during roasting. The fat skin-covered neck cavity sticks up into the air. The breast sits on its large cavity in its pan and creates the hollow in which the heat can circulate to cook the meat faster.

Lay the disjointed drumstick-thigh pieces skin-side up (and underside salted) in the same pan with the breast. If an additional oven is available, these pieces can be roasted separately in another

---

*It is very important to note that oven temperatures tend to vary in each stove. Therefore, it is essential that you determine the accuracy of your oven temperature. Oven thermometers are available at all cookware stores. Remember that your oven dial does not necessarily reflect the oven's true temperature.

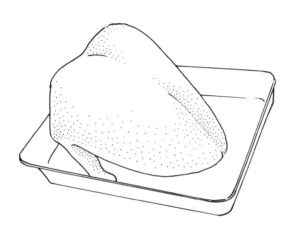

Trimmed breast, in self-basting position, ready for the oven.

oiled pan. This is especially helpful when using the larger birds.

Put the turkey into the oven, adjust the temperature to 350° F, and begin timing. The breast of a large 22- to 24-pound tom turkey still on the carcass, along with the drumstick-thigh pieces, will now cook in approximately 2-1/4 hours.

After roasting for 2-1/4 hours, the turkey pieces should be removed from the oven. Remember that no roast should be carved immediately upon removal from the oven. For this size turkey, a minimum of 20 minutes for "setting" or recirculation is absolutely essential. (This allows the juices to redistribute themselves and equalize their pressure and heat throughout the tissues of the

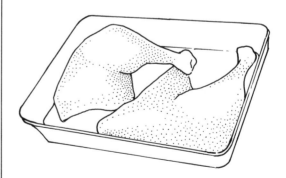

Thigh-drumstick pieces ready for the oven.

49

USING THE MEAT THERMOMETER

1. Use only professional style thermometers which have only degrees marked on the dial.
2. When the approximate roasting time has been reached, remove the roast and its pan from the oven and search out the thickest part of the meat.
3. Insert the thermometer quickly in the center of the thickest part and take a reading at once.
4. Push the thermometer further in and take a reading, then pull it further out from the original point of reading to take another reading. The lowest of the three readings is the correct one on which to proceed.
5. If the temperature specified in the recipe has been reached, commence the setting time. If the roast is not yet at the proper temperature, put it back in the oven and check at regular intervals. Remember that the last 10 degrees of increase in temperature will be achieved very quickly. A roast that checks at 125° F may need only 5 minutes more in the oven to reach the proper temperature.
6. If the roast is overcooked, place it on a cold plate and in a cool spot to prevent further heat penetration.

meat.) During the first 10 minutes at room temperature, the roast stops cooking. During the next 10 minutes, the roast may be kept in a warming oven that does not exceed 140° F. At higher temperatures, the roasting process will continue. The roast may be kept in the warming oven for up to 1/2 hour more without a loss of quality.

To reassemble the breast and drumstick-thigh pieces on a plat- ter for presentation, place the breast, crop-side up, in the center of the plate. Position the drumstick-thighs on each side in as natural a position as possible. Garnish with small bunches of parsley and cherry tomatoes.

CHAPTER THREE

TECHNIQUE:
BONING THE BREAST
AND THIGH

When you wish to serve both light and dark turkey meat as a roast that you can prepare quickly and serve easily, and you do not wish to present a "whole" turkey at the table, then boning the breast and thigh before you cook sticks, half breast, and center sections of the wings for later use.

Boning and then roasting the half breast and one thigh for 35 to 40 minutes still enables you to make a delicious gravy prepared from the pan drippings (see p. 130). You can prepare the stuffing of your

---

"Americans sometimes have too cavalier an approach to food—they do not use up all the parts. It is because many of them have never known hunger." **KW**

---

them is the logical choice. By using the following technique, you will have 14 to 16 servings from one thigh and half the breast of a 22- to 24-pound turkey. You can freeze the remaining thigh, two drumchoice on the side (see pp. 140 and 142).

Slice the roasted turkey without ceremony in the kitchen and attractively arrange it on a serving platter, or carve it easily at the table as your

★ ★

guests state their preferences for dark or light meat. With a sharp carving knife, slicing the boned turkey makes even the most inexperienced carver seem expert, the more demanding cutting having been done before the roasting.

REMOVING AND BONING THE THIGH

First disjoint the turkey as directed in Chapter 1. Then proceed as follows.

Separate the thigh from the drumstick by cutting through the "knee" joint. Locate the connecting ligaments between the two bones, cut them, and continue to cut through the flesh, separating the two parts. Reserve the drumstick for another meal.

1

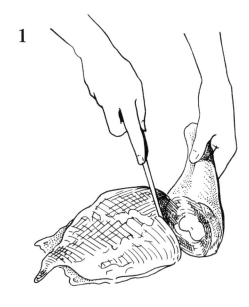

Remove thigh from drumstick by cutting through "knee" joint.

Place the thigh skin-side down. With the tip of your boning knife, cut along the side of the bone, following it the full length from the top to the bottom on both sides of

2

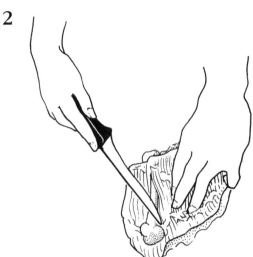

3

Follow the full length of the thigh bone with the tip of your knife from the top to the bottom of the bone on both sides.

Slip knife under bone at point halfway down its length. Cut to top of bone.

the bone. When the bone becomes visible, slip the knife under it at a point halfway down its length. Cutting away from yourself, free the top end of the bone from the flesh.

Turn the thigh around, lift the free end of the bone with one hand, and cut the other end free. Reserve the bone for stock.

Even though you may not be

★ ★

BONING THE BREAST

To remove both sides of the breast from the carcass (as cut from the back, p. 38), place the carcass on the cutting board, breast up, resting on the ends of the attached upper wing joints (first section of the wings).

Insert the tip of the boning knife at the V-point of the wishbone and the breastbone or *keel*. Make one long cut along one side of the keel all the way down. Repeat on the other side of the keel.

Then, insert the tip of the boning knife, again at the V-point. With the cutting edge of the blade away from you, cut upward through the center of the skin of the crop to further separate the two sides of the breast.

For complete separation, cut through the socket at the shoulder near the wishbone, freeing the

4

Free top end of bone from flesh.

using it for this meal, it would be a good idea at this time to bone the other thigh as well.

wing from the carcass on each side. Then hold the breast firmly by the wing bone and cut one side completely free from the carcass by following the bone structure of the rib cage with the tip of the boning knife, turning it over and working from the back side as needed. Repeat for the other side. Now you should have two breast sections, each with the upper (first joint) wing attached. Use the boned carcass for stock.

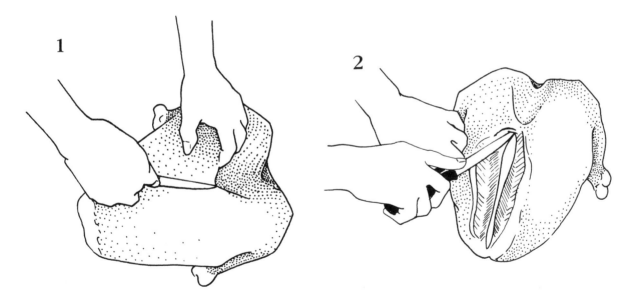

1 Insert tip of boning knife at V-point.

2 Cut along both sides of the keel.

3

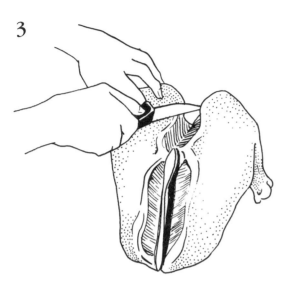

4

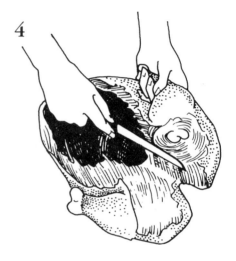

With cutting edge away from you, insert tip of knife at V-point and cut upward through center of skin of crop.

Cut through socket at shoulder near wishbone, freeing wing on each side. Hold breast firmly by wing bone and cut one side completely free from carcass by following bone structure of rib cage with tip of knife, turning breast over and working from the back side as needed.

ROASTING

Place one breast piece and one thigh, well salted, on the cut side, skin-side up, in a well-oiled, low-sided roasting pan. Preheat the oven to 450° F, but roast at 375° F for 35 to 40 minutes. Allow 10 to 15 minutes for recirculation time at room temperature before carving. Serve with all the usual trimmings.

CHAPTER FOUR

TECHNIQUE: LARDING AND ROASTING THE BREAST

I t is the fat in meat tissues that supplies flavor and keeps the meat juicy as it roasts. With a very low-fat meat like turkey—particularly the white meat of the breast—it is often desirable to supply additional fat. This is especially true if the skin has been removed. A classic and elegant way to do this is by larding.

will find that larding is not at all difficult. Larding creates an attractive pattern and a much more effective penetration of the fat which enables it to do its taste-improving work without melting off.

Plain pork back fat, firm and unsalted, works best because it has a low melting point, very pleasing flavor, is easy to digest, and is read-

---

"I really don't want to give you a big buildup on this, BUT . . ." **KW**

Larding is the process of inserting tiny "logs" of fat by threading them into the meat. It is a more advanced technique than barding, which is the tying of a layer of fat over or around a piece of meat. With some practice, however, you

ily available. You may also use salt pork fat and slab bacon fat; the lean parts may be reserved for other uses, such as in the dressing.

A good larding needle is essential. This instrument is a long, pointed metal tube which is split at the large end. The split holds the little logs of fat and permits them to be threaded deep into the meat. Although many styles of larding needles are available, I have found that the most practical needle is one made in France which has a simple four-way split at the large end. (See illustration.) The more complicated (and often more expensive) larding needles with hinges or other adjustments do not work as smoothly as the French model.

Cut chilled fat into little logs—1/8 inch × 1/8 inch × 2 inches.

The lardons must fit into the split end of the needle, so the accuracy of the cut is important. Keep the lardons chilled if you are working slowly in a hot kitchen.

LARDING THE TURKEY BREAST

Cutting the lardons Partially freeze the fat to facilitate cutting. Cut the pork fat into 1/8-inch slabs and then into 1/8-inch by 2-inch logs. These are known by their French name, *lardons.*

Preparing the breast Bone the breast (two halves) by the method described in Chapter 3 (p. 58). Cut off the upper wing joints. Remove the skin from the breasts by lifting

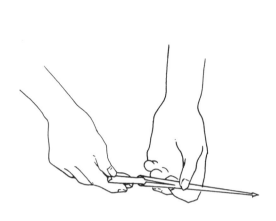

Fit chilled lardon into split end of needle.

Insert lardons evenly parallel to grain of meat 1/2 to 3/4 inch apart.

the skin carefully and using the tip of your boning knife to assist in the separation. The parts may be reserved for other dishes.

Larding Larding should be done in neat rows on the top side of the meat where the skin was, parallel to the grain.

Insert the lardons evenly, about 1/2 inch to 3/4 inch apart. (See il-lustration.) One-third of each lardon should protrude from the insertion point, one-third should be in the meat, and one-third should protrude at the exit end. The process can be likened to the act of inserting a safety pin.

Lard the whole of the top surface of each breast half.

Roasting Preheat the oven to 400° F. Salt the larded breasts on both sides and place them, larded-side up, into an oiled, low-sided pan.

Place the pan on the rack in the upper third of the preheated oven and roast at 350° F for 15 minutes. Reduce the heat to 300° F and continue to roast for 25 minutes more.

Remove from the oven and allow to set at room temperature for 10 minutes before slicing, to recirculate juices and equalize their pressure and heat. This time period will allow you to make your gravy or sauce. (See Chapter 8.)

Lard boneless, skinless thighs in the same manner. However, reduce their roasting time to 20 minutes total and 7 to 8 minutes recirculation time at room temperature.

CHAPTER FIVE

A CLASSIC UPDATED— THE ROULADE

As you become more adept and courageous in your handling of the turkey, not only can you shorten the traditional 6-hour stuffing and roasting and carving-at-the-table syndrome for the "whole" bird (see Chapter 2), but you can also begin realize one of the elegant variations possible with turkey. A roulade is a layered roll which you will prepare and handle much as you would a jelly roll. It requires much time and perseverance, of course, but improvement (and gastronomic delight) comes with each experience.

"In our profession, gourmet cooking is believed to mean something very complicated. We'll see." **KW**

---

to explore the many classic and more elegant adaptations for this delicious meat.

ROULADE

The preparation of a roulade offers the serious cook an opportunity to

As was pointed out in the introduction, this is a book of techniques. Here, you will be making good use of your skills with a knife to debone the meat for the roulade. The completely boneless white and dark meat, the eye appeal of the spiral pattern when the roulade is sliced, and the added flavor of a fresh vegetable within the roast make this an unusual and outstanding example of today's modern version of the classic ballotine.

When purchasing the cabbage, be sure to select a head that has deep, dark-green outer leaves. Such leaves supply an attractive contrast to the white breast meat.

1 half turkey breast, uncooked, boned, and skinned (see p. 59 and p. 64)

1 turkey thigh, uncooked, boned (see p. 56), skinned, and well chilled

Skin from both pieces (as intact as possible)

1 large, curly-leafed cabbage (Savoy cabbage)

Salt

White pepper

1/4 teaspoon ground ginger

1/4 teaspoon allspice

2 egg whites, well chilled or partially frozen

1/2 cup Turkey Stock (see p. 122), defatted and well chilled or partially frozen

Cotton twine

Oil

Prepare the turkey pieces. (Refer to the techniques described on pp. 58 through 59 and p. 64 for boning and skinning the meat. Be sure to remove the attached upper wing, as for preparing the breast for larding. Skin the thigh the same way you skin the breast.) The skin of both pieces will serve as the final wrap for the roulade, so be careful to keep it as intact as possible.

Remove eight to ten of the outer dark leaves of the cabbage and parboil them in salted water until they are limp. Drain and lay the leaves flat, side by side, on a cloth towel, cover with another towel, and roll over all with a rolling pin. This will allow the towels to absorb the water left on the leaves. Set aside.

The filling Coarsely chop the chilled thigh. Puree the chilled meat in a food processor until it becomes a fine paste. Add the spices and the partially frozen egg whites. Continue to process for 1 minute more to make a smooth paste. Then add the partially frozen stock and blend well. Set aside.

Preparing the breast Lay out the breast and remove the filet. (See illustration.)

Butterfly-cut the breast in as many places as necessary until it becomes a rectangle, approximately 10 inches by 14 inches.

Cover the meat with a sheet of plastic wrap and carefully pound it, using a rolling pin or the flat side of a cleaver. Do not use the textured points of a meat tenderizer. If you

Making the Roulade

1

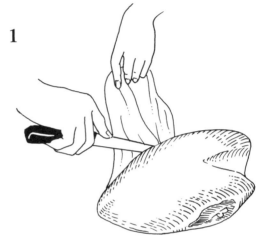

Remove skin from breast.

2

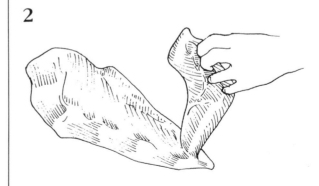

Remove filet.

3

Butterfly-cut breast in as many places as necessary until it becomes a rectangle, approximately 10 inches × 14 inches.

4

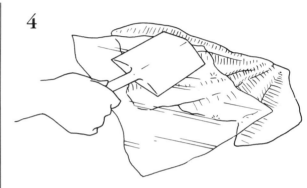

Cover with plastic wrap and, pounding with a flat tool, shape to uniform thickness.

must use this tool, turn it so you are pounding with the flat side. Pound and shape the breast to a uniform thickness, making a slightly larger rectangle than the one with which you began.

Pound the filet separately and use it to fill in the rectangular shape or to lay over the thinner parts of the meat.

To assemble Preheat the oven to 400° F.

Spread out a large rectangular sheet of aluminum foil, oil it, and arrange the pounded rectangle of breast meat on it. Salt and pepper it.

Take half the prepared dark-meat filling and spread it evenly over the entire breast. Apply a layer of cabbage leaves, overlapping generously to cover the filling. Do not allow the leaves to extend over the edges of the meat. Spread the remaining filling over the cabbage leaves.

Start rolling as you would a jelly roll on the long side of the meat, keeping the roll as tight as possible. Use the foil to assist and lift in the rolling.

Place the sheet of reserved turkey skin over the top of the roll and tuck it under the sides, covering the roll as completely as possible. With cotton twine, tie the roll in as many intervals and as close together as is necessary to keep its loglike shape. Sprinkle lightly with salt and brush with oil.

Transfer the roulade to an oiled, low-sided pan and roast in a preheated oven at 400° F for 15 minutes or until the skin is well browned. Then reduce the heat to 350° F and

5

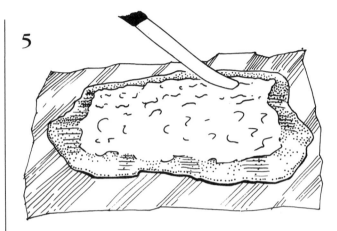

Arrange on oiled foil. Salt and pepper and spread dark meat filling evenly over breast.

6

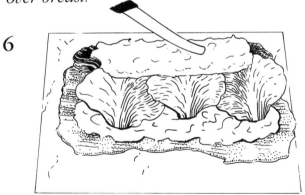

Arrange layer of cabbage leaves to cover filling and spread them with remaining filling.

7

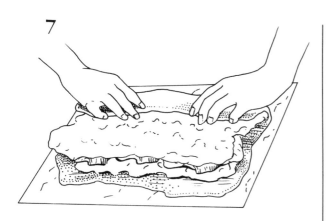

Start rolling as you would a jelly roll on long side of meat. Use foil to assist.

continue to roast for a *total* roasting time of no more than 30 minutes. Remove the roulade from the oven.

During the essential recirculation time of 15 minutes between the time the roast is taken from the oven and the time it can be sliced, the sauce or gravy can be made. (See Chapter 8.)

Makes 14 to 16 slices.

8

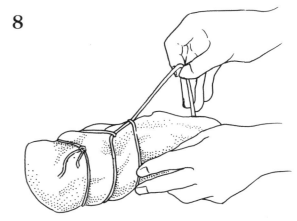

With cotton twine, tie roll to keep its loglike shape.

9

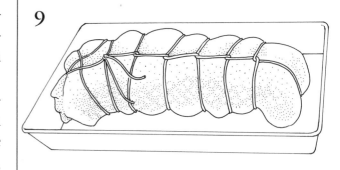

Oiled, salted roulade ready for baking.

RECIPES FOR EVERY DAY

When the various parts of a large tom turkey are assembled after disjointing and dividing as described in Chapter 1, there is an almost endless variety of dishes waiting to be prepared and at a fraction of the cost of purchasing the parts separately. Almost nothing is wasted. The yield of edible meat is a high 60 percent— higher than chicken, beef, pork, or lamb. (Lamb yields only 35 percent.) So, choose your favorite turkey parts and prepare low-cost, low-fat, high-protein dishes every day, not just at holiday time. Remember that the recipes that follow are all based on parts from a large 22- to 24-pound tom turkey.

The suggested roasting times are on the next page. Their internal temperature before roasting should not be lower than 60° F. It is important that after roasting, a setting or recirculation time of 25 to 30 percent of the roasting time be observed.

> *"Turkey tastes perhaps more pronounced or gamier than chicken, but it is still neutral enough to blend into most preparations suitable for other meats."* KW

Cut	Approximate Roasting Time	Oven Temp.	Takeout Internal Temp.	Setting Time
Two breasts on carcass with first wing joints and two drumstick-thighs	2 hrs., 15 min.	350°F	Breast 143°F Drum-thigh 160°F	30 min.
Boned breast with first wing joint and all skin on	35–45 min.	375°F	143°F	10 min.
Boned breast, wing off, skin off, larded or unlarded	40–50 min.	325°F	143°F	10 min.
Drumstick and thigh only, bone in	1 hr., 15 min.	350°F	160°F	20 min.
Drumstick only, bone in	1 hr.	350°F	160°F	15 min.

BREAST

Here are instructions for preparing the breast for the recipes that follow.

Place the deboned and skinned breast (pp. 59 and 64), without the upper wing joint, with the skinned-side down on a cutting surface. Remove the filet-shaped part of the breast, which is already loose. Set aside.

Cut the remaining large piece, starting at the large end, into three equal pieces, cutting as closely with the grain as possible.

Each of these pieces can now be cut across the grain (i.e., at right angles to the previous cuts). Depending on the thickness of the slab, you can make scallopine 1/2 inch thick (three per serving), medallions 1 inch thick (two per serving), or cutlets 1-1/2 inches thick (one per serving). Lay the slices on the cutting board. Cover with a sheet of plastic wrap and flatten by pounding gently with the flat side of a cleaver. The pieces should be pounded to a bit less than 1/4 inch thick.

Making Scallopine, Medallions, and Cutlets ⟶

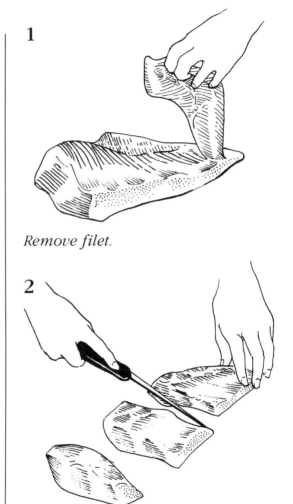

1

Remove filet.

2

Cut large piece of breast, starting at large end, into three equal pieces.

3

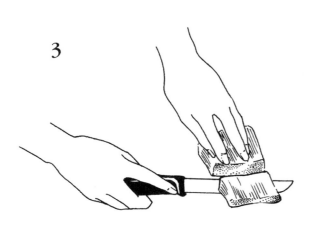

Each of the three pieces can be cut across the grain.

4

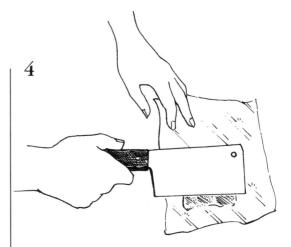

Cover with sheet of plastic wrap and pound gently with flat side of cleaver.

Rollatine

This recipe for little turkey rolls stresses freshness of ingredients and flavor as well as ease of preparation.

Tomates Concassées Sauce (see p. 132)
8 turkey breast medallions (see p. 78), pounded thin
Salt
3 cups spinach leaves, blanched, coarsely chopped, and squeezed dry
1/2 cup ricotta cheese
1/2 cup dry feta cheese, crumbled
Zest of 1 lemon
Pepper
8 strips lean bacon

Prepare the Tomates Concassées Sauce and set aside, keeping it warm.

Place the medallions side by side on a large surface and salt lightly.

In a bowl, combine the spinach, ricotta, feta, and lemon zest. Add salt and pepper to taste and mix thoroughly.

Divide the mixture equally for the number of medallions used. Shape the mixture into little logs and place one on each medallion. Roll into little rolls (rollatine). Spiral a strip of bacon around each roll. Arrange the rolls on a broiler pan, making sure the end of each bacon wrap is on the underside. Broil 3 inches from the heat for 6 to 8 minutes. Turn the broiler off.

Remove the pan from its broiling position and place it on the lowest rack possible. Close the oven door and allow the rollatine to remain undisturbed in the oven for 3 to 5 minutes more.

To serve, spoon Tomates Concassées Sauce on each individual plate and top with one roll.

Serves 8.

Cutlets with Basil and Gruyère

The nutty flavor of a fine Swiss Gruyère cheese, melted with the sweet flavor of basil, makes this a simple celebration of flavors. Serve it with a light, fruity white wine.

6 raw turkey breast cutlets
  (see p. 78)

(see p. 78)

Salt

3 eggs, beaten

6 slices Gruyère cheese, approx-
  imately 2 inches by 4 inches

2 tablespoons fresh basil, chopped
  (or 1 tablespoon dried basil if fresh
  is not in season)

Flour

Oil for frying

Lemon wedges

Parsley

Pound the cutlets into very thin squares approximately 6 inches by 6 inches and salt them. Brush half of the upper surface of each cutlet with beaten egg. Place a slice of cheese on the egg-coated section of each cutlet, aligning it so its long side is along what will be the fold across the center of the cutlet. Sprinkle 1 teaspoon fresh basil (or 1/2 teaspoon dried) on each piece of cheese and fold the uncoated half of each cutlet over it, matching the three cut edges to the lower layer. Pat the three edges to seal and enclose the cheese in the folded cutlets securely. Place them on a tray until ready to serve.

At serving time, heat a dry skillet. Dip the folded cutlets into flour and coat both sides. Shake off the excess flour and dip the cutlets into beaten egg. Coat both sides evenly with the egg.

Put a small amount of oil into the hot, dry skillet. As soon as the oil begins to smoke, place the egg-dipped cutlets into the hot oil and sauté quickly, no longer than 1 minute on each side. Serve at once.

Garnish with lemon wedges and parsley and serve with home-fried potatoes.

Serves 6.

Turkey Breast Provençal

Here is a recipe of our editor's that makes use of the flavors of Provence: garlic, anchovies, olives, olive oil, and tomatoes. We suggest serving it with the Venetian rice dish, *risi e bisi.**

1 onion, coarsely cut

1/2 bunch cilantro, coarsely cut

6 stalks celery, coarsely cut

1 bay leaf

1 turkey breast, deboned (see p. 59), skinless (see p. 64), and tied to hold in the filet

8 cups (or more, as needed) Turkey Stock (see p. 122), boiling

3 anchovy filets

4 cloves garlic, chopped

4 tablespoons olive oil

1 onion, minced

1-1/2 tablespoons tomato paste

5 tomatoes, peeled, deseeded, and roughly chopped

1 red or yellow bell pepper, cut into strips

1-1/2 cups dry white wine

1 teaspoon dried oregano

Several basil leaves, chopped

Pepper

Salt

Zest of one lemon, finely grated

2/3 cup Niçoise olives

1/2 cup parsley, finely chopped

Place the coarsely cut onion, cilantro, celery, and bay leaf in a stockpot large enough to hold the breast. Lay the tied breast on top of the vegetables, cover generously with boiling Turkey Stock, and bring to a simmer. Continue to simmer until the breast is tender, approximately 1 hour.

Mash two anchovy filets and the garlic together. Sauté the resulting paste in 2 tablespoons olive oil in a heavy skillet

---

*Make *risi e bisi* by boiling 1-1/2 cups raw white rice in Turkey Stock, then tossing with 1-1/2 cups fresh peas.

with the minced onion until the onion pieces are translucent. Add the tomato paste and stir over a high heat until the tomato paste begins to caramelize at the bottom of the pan. Add the tomatoes, bell pepper, wine, oregano, basil, and pepper and salt to taste. Put a pinch of the lemon zest in the sauce and simmer and reduce until the sauce is quite thick. Add the olives. Mix the rest of the zest with the parsley and set aside.

After the turkey breast has cooked, slice thinly and arrange on a serving platter. Pour the sauce over the slices. Rinse the remaining anchovy filet, split it up the middle, and garnish the dish lengthwise with the anchovy filet halves. Drizzle the remaining olive oil over all and top with the lemon zest and parsley mixture.

Serves 6 to 8.

Marinated Breast in Sour Cream

The spicy marinade in which this turkey breast soaks was originally developed as a preservative. Its tangy flavor is complemented by the rich sauce.

2 cups dry white wine
2 cups Turkey Stock (see p. 122)
Juice and zest of 1 lemon

MIREPOIX CONSISTING OF THE FOLLOWING, COARSELY CHOPPED:
   1 onion
   6 stalks celery

1 carrot

1/2 bunch parsley

1 teaspoon pickling spices, crushed

10 juniper berries, crushed

1 turkey breast, boneless (see p. 59), skinless (see p. 64), larded (see p. 64) or unlarded, and lightly salted

1 cup sour cream

2 tablespoons flour

1 cup Turkey Velouté Sauce (see p. 131)

1 tablespoon dill weed, dried

In a saucepan, combine the wine, Turkey Stock, lemon juice and zest, *mirepoix*, pickling spices, and juniper berries. Bring to a boil, lower the heat, and simmer for 2 minutes. Cool completely.

Place the breast in a narrow, non-oxydizing container (glass, china, or stainless steel), and pour the cool, spiced stock over it. Cover the container with plastic wrap to seal, and refrigerate for 2 to 4 days.

After at least 2, but no more than 4, days, place the meat and its marinade into a stainless steel saucepan and simmer at 180° to 190° F for about 1 hour. Do not boil.

Remove the meat and keep warm. Strain the liquid into a clean saucepan. Combine the sour cream with the flour and add it to the liquid along with the Velouté Sauce. Blend well and check for seasoning. Add more wine and stock as needed and keep hot.

Slice the meat, arrange it on a serving platter, and spoon the sauce over it, reserving the remainder of the sauce to be served on the side. Sprinkle with dill and serve with a fluffy baked potato.

Serves 8 to 10.

Almond-Crusted Medallions

This dish is absolutely unique. Although I have served it for many years, I have never found its duplicate in any book or on any table.

8 medallions (see p. 78) of turkey breast
Salt
1/4 cup flour
2 eggs, well beaten
1 cup sliced almonds, blanched
1-1/2 sticks butter
1 lemon
Watercress
Lemon wedges

Prepare the medallions; pound and salt them.

Arrange three shallow bowls or pie pans side by side.

If you are right-handed, use the following sequence, or reverse it if you are left-handed. Put the flour in the left pan, the eggs in the center pan, and the almonds in the pan on the right.

With your left hand, dip a medallion into the flour. Turn to coat well, shake off the excess flour, and lay it in the egg pan, coating only one side. Still using your left hand, remove the medallion from the egg, drain off any excess egg, and place the medallion, coated side down, into the almonds.

With your dry right hand, pat the upper (floured) side to press the almonds into the lower (egg-coated) side. Lift and place it almond-side-up on an un-greased jelly roll pan or baking sheet. Rearrange almonds (if necessary) so they cover the medallion in an even layer.

Repeat with each medallion and lay them side by side on the baking pan. (Whether you are preparing this or any other breaded dish, if you follow this sequence, you will always have a free dry hand with which to work.)

The preparation can be done several hours in advance. The meat, however, should be covered with plastic wrap and refrigerated until sautéed.

At serving time, melt 1/2 stick butter in a skillet large enough to hold four medallions. Place four medallions almond-side-down in the hot butter and sauté over a medium heat until the almonds are golden. Turn carefully and sauté 1 minute longer. Remove to a heat-proof platter and keep warm in a low oven or a warmer. Melt another 1/2 stick butter and sauté the second batch of medallions.

To serve, arrange all the medallions on a serving platter, almond-side-up. Squeeze the juice of half a lemon over all.

In a small skillet, melt the remaining 1/2 stick of butter until it foams and pour over all the meat. Garnish with watercress and lemon wedges.

Serves 4.

Turkey Scallopine
with Capers and Chardonnay

1 cup Turkey Velouté Sauce (see p. 131)
12 turkey breast scallopine (see p. 78)
Salt
Flour
3 ounces unsalted* butter
1/2 cup dry Chardonnay
*2 tablespoons capers, coarsely
  chopped in their own juice*
1 tablespoon parsley, minced

Prepare the Turkey Velouté Sauce and set aside.

Prepare the turkey breast scallopine (see p. 78). Pound, then lightly salt them. Dip the scallopine in flour, coating both sides.

In a 10-inch skillet, melt half the butter. When the butter is hot, sauté four to six scallopine for 1/2 minute on each side. Remove them to a heatproof platter and keep them warm while you sauté the remaining scallopine in the rest of the butter. Remove all the scallopine to the platter.

Immediately pour the wine and the Velouté Sauce into the skillet, and deglaze (see p. 24), reducing to a smooth sauce.

Add the capers and the accumulated juices from the scallopine platter. Stir well and bring to a boil. Remove from the heat, return the presautéed scallopine (and any remaining juices) to the pan and add the parsley. Mix well and serve immediately.

Plain buttered tagliatelle or plain steamed potatoes go quite well with this dish.

Serves 4.

---

*It may seem inconsistent to specify unsalted butter even though the meat has been salted. However, when you salt your own meat, you know just how much salt you have used. Also, ordinary salted butter contains a larger amount of water and less butter fat than unsalted butter. This makes for a discernable difference in the consistency of your sauce.

Turkey
Cutlets Milanese

These cutlets can be breaded several hours before serving if they are wrapped and refrigerated. At serving time, pan-fry them quickly so they may be served at the peak of their flavor and freshness.

Spicy Tomato Sauce (see p. 134)
4 turkey breast cutlets, pounded (see
 p. 78)
Salt
Flour
2 eggs, beaten
Bread crumbs
Fat for frying (oil, bacon fat, pork
 fat, etc.)
Few sprigs parsley
Lemon slices

Prepare the Spicy Tomato Sauce and set aside.

Prepare the cutlets and salt them lightly. Using the breading technique explained in the recipe for Almond-Crusted Medallions (p. 86), dip the cut lets first into the flour, then the eggs, and finally into the bread crumbs, coating both sides well.

Choose a skillet large enough to accommodate the cutlets comfortably. Use enough frying fat so the cutlets will not stick and heat it so that loose bread crumbs sizzle when dropped into the fat. Do not allow the fat to reach smoking point.

Lower each cutlet carefully into the hot fat, taking care not to splash. Shake the pan lightly and, with a cooking fork, move the cutlets gently about in the skillet. Move frequently to prevent sticking and burning. After 1 minute or a few seconds longer, the bottom sides should be golden brown.

Turn each cutlet and fry the other side. When the other sides are equally golden, remove the cutlets from the pan and place on paper towels to absorb all traces of fat. *continued...*

Pour several small ladles of hot Spicy Tomato Sauce onto a heated platter, arrange the cutlets on top, garnish with parsley and slices of lemon, and serve at once.

Serves 4.

Stir-Fry
with Bok Choy
and Green Onions

This simple Chinese stir-fry is an excellent way to use the trimmings from boning the breast or cutting scallopine, medallions, and cutlets.

Salt

2 to 3 cups raw breast trimmings, sliced across the grain as thin as possible

2 cloves garlic, minced

1 teaspoon grated ginger

Hot pepper flakes

Peanut oil

1 cup Turkey Stock (see p. 122), cold and defatted

2 to 3 tablespoons soy sauce

1 tablespoon sugar

2 to 3 tablespoons cornstarch

2 bunches green onions, including most of the green stems, washed and sliced diagonally in 1/4-inch slices

1 small head bok choy (or Napa cabbage), washed and thinly cut

Sesame oil

Salt the raw meat slices. In a bowl, mix the garlic, ginger, and pepper flakes with 2 tablespoons peanut oil and toss the meat to coat well. Allow to marinate at least 1 hour.

In another bowl, mix the cold Turkey Stock with the soy sauce, sugar, and cornstarch. Stir to blend in the cornstarch and set aside.

Heat a wok or large skillet and add enough peanut oil to cover the bottom and sides. Sauté the onions for 1 minute. Add the bok choy and salt to taste.

Cover and allow to cook for no longer than 3 minutes. Remove the vegetables from the wok and keep warm.

Rinse or wipe the wok, reheat, and add a little oil. Toss in the marinated meat and stir-fry quickly. Add a few drops of sesame oil, then the onions and cabbage.

Stir the soy sauce mixture well and pour it over the meat and vegetables. Bring to a good boil and turn off the heat.

Serve with cooked rice.

Serves 4.

Turkey Tzimmes

Tzimmes means *fuss* or *excitement* in Yiddish, the implication being that one makes a *tzimmes* when someone special is coming to dinner.

Salt
5 cups breast meat, cubed
1/2 cup olive oil
1/2 pound California dried prunes, pitted, quartered
1/2 pound California dried apricots, quartered
3 cups Turkey Stock (see p. 122)
1/2 cup onions, minced
3 tablespoons flour
1/4 cup honey
1/2 tablespoon fresh ginger, chopped
1/4 teaspoon ground cloves
1/4 teaspoon ground cinnamon
6 sweet potatoes, baked

Lightly salt the cubed meat and toss to coat in 2 tablespoons of the oil.

In a saucepan, cover the dried fruits with the Turkey Stock, bring to a boil, reduce the heat, and simmer until the fruits are tender but still firm. Drain the fruit, reserving the fruited stock liquid.

Heat a large skillet and sauté the onions in the remaining oil. Stir in the flour to make a roux. Deglaze the pan with the fruited stock. Add the honey, ginger, cloves, and cinnamon. Bring to a boil and keep warm.

Heat a skillet and sauté the oiled meat cubes (perhaps in two or three lots) in the remaining oil for 1 minute for each batch. Remove to a stainless steel bowl and keep warm. When all the meat is sautéed and removed from the skillet, add the finished sauce and return the meat and its juices to the skillet.

Add the cooked fruits and reheat to boiling. Check for seasoning.

Serve with a freshly baked, split sweet potato for each person.

Serves 6.

Spaghetti Angela

This is an unusual northern Italian-style pasta dish: it is light, white, and richly flavored. It is another delicious way to use the trimmings from boning the breast or cutting scallopine, medallions, and cutlets.

3-1/2 quarts water

1 tablespoon salt

1 pound spaghetti (or any pasta such as spaghettini, tagliarini, or fettucini)

1 stick butter

1/2 cup onions, finely minced

1 cup raw mushrooms, fresh, white, coarsley ground

2 cups raw breast trimmings, coarsely ground in a processor

1 cup frozen green peas, defrosted

2 cups Turkey Velouté Sauce (see p. 131)

1 cup heavy cream

Parmesan cheese, freshly grated

In a 1-gallon kettle, bring the water and salt to a fast boil and cook the pasta *al dente*. Drain, rinse with cold water, and drain again. Set aside.

In a large saucepan, melt 1/2 stick butter until it foams. Add the onions and sauté briefly. Add the mushrooms and the ground meat. Stir and continue to sauté for 30 seconds.

Add the peas, Velouté Sauce, and cream. Bring to a good boil and taste for salt. Adjust seasoning if necessary.

In a large skillet, reheat pasta in 1/2 stick hot butter. Arrange on a heated platter, spoon the hot sauce over it, and sprinkle generously with grated Parmesan cheese. Serve at once.

Serves 4.

Turkey Sandwich

The French keep their sandwiches simple, the key being their use of a few fine ingredients. The following is our editor, Maggie Klein's, suggestion, for making a French-style sandwich that will have you smelling like southern France for days. It is quite simple: use one long, crusty sweet baguette; pumate (sun-dried tomatoes stored in olive oil) sliced thin; a little less than a pound of turkey breast meat, roasted or poached, sliced *very* thin; and a slathering of the following recipe for aïoli. (Aïoli is the thick, garlicky mayonnaise from Provence.) You may want to reduce the number of garlic cloves.

Aïoli

4 cloves fresh garlic, crushed

1/2 tablespoon dry bread crumbs

White wine vinegar

1 egg yolk (or two if the eggs are small)

1 cup fine olive oil

Salt

In a bowl with a curved bottom, mix the crushed garlic with the bread crumbs and moisten with a few drops of vinegar. Add the egg yolk and beat with a wire whisk until the yolk is light yellow. Add the olive oil a drop at a time for the first few tablespoons of oil, beating while you add it, then increase the rate of addition to a fine drizzle until all the oil is added and you have a thick mayonnaise. Salt to taste.

Breast Sauté
with Feta and Tomatoes

Even though the taste of feta cheese (made from sheep's milk) may remind you of Greek-style dishes, feta-type cheeses are made in many countries now and have become a favorite fresh flavoring ingredient for a variety of dishes.

4 cups turkey breast meat, thinly sliced and salted

2 tablespoons olive oil

1/2 cup onions, minced

1/2 stick butter, melted

1 cup dry white wine

1/4 teaspoon dried tarragon

3 cups Turkey Velouté Sauce (see p. 131)

2 large tomatoes, peeled, cut in half, and deseeded

1/4 pound feta cheese, cut into 1/2-inch cubes

2 tablespoons chives, chopped

Toss the salted meat slices in the olive oil and set aside.

In a skillet, sauté the onions in the melted butter. Cook until transparent. Deglaze the skillet with the wine, tarragon, and Velouté Sauce. Cook to reduce for 5 to 10 minutes. Strain and keep warm. You should have about 2 cups of smooth, heavy sauce.

Cut each of the tomato halves into eight pieces and drain.

Five minutes before serving, heat a dry 12-inch skillet to very hot and add the oiled meat slices. Sauté briefly—no more than 30 seconds. Add the drained tomato pieces and the sauce. Stir well and bring to a boil. Remove from the heat, add the feta cubes, and check the seasoning.

Serve sprinkled with the chives. Plain buttered pasta makes a good companion dish.

Serves 4.

Boudin Blanc

Literally, *boudin blanc* means *white pudding*, but it is the term generally used in American specialty food stores for delicate white sausages. In the following recipe, Maggie Klein has adapted her recipe for *boudin blanc* to be made with turkey breast meat. The result is a tender, succulent, and delicate sausage. You may wish to double the recipe and serve sausages the next day.

About 30 inches sausage casing
1/2 pound turkey breast meat, well trimmed and chopped
1/2 pound pork back fat, chopped
1 onion, chopped
1 egg
5 ounces heavy cream
1/2 tablespoon salt
1 teaspoon white pepper
2 tablespoons parsley, minced
1 tablespoon dried chervil
Cotton twine

Rinse the salt from the sausage casing, soak in water, and set aside.

Put the turkey breast, pork fat, and onion into a processor and process until the mixture is homogenous.

With a whisk, mix the egg, cream, and seasoning until well blended. Add the mixture to the processor. Process until well mixed.

Set up your meat grinder and attach the sausage device. Find the end of the casing and feed the casing onto the sausage attachment. Put some of the meat mixture into the grinder and begin turning the crank. After all the air bubbles are forced out of the casing (after about an inch of meat is expelled), tie the casing and continue to grind until all the meat mixture is in the casing.

Tie the other end of the casing, then make equal-sized sausages by tying the casing at regular intervals.

★★★★★★★★★★★★★★★★★★★★★★★★★★★★★★★

Cook the sausages in a skillet with 1/2 inch of water. When the sausages have become firm, you may cut them apart. Poke the sausages with a sharp fork to allow the juices to escape. Turn the sausages once while the water is evaporating. After the water has evaporated from the pan, add a little oil and brown the sausages on both sides.

Makes 6 sausages.

★★★★★★★★★★★★★★★★★★★★★★★★★★★★★★★

Roasted Drumsticks

Preheat the oven to 350° F.

Wash two drumsticks; do not dry. Rub 1 teaspoon of salt on each drumstick. Place in a well-oiled pan with low sides. Brush the top of the drumsticks with oil.

Bake in a preheated oven at 350° F for 1 hour and 15 minutes. No basting is necessary. It is important that the oven door remain closed during the roasting period. Each time you open the oven door to check on the meat, the oven temperature drops and you will only prolong the roasting time.

Serve as roasted drumsticks or remove the meat from the bones and dice, slice, or cut as required for the recipe you will use.

Turkey Mole

The unusual ingredients for this Mexican turkey in chocolate sauce can be found in your local Mexican grocery. This is one of our editor's favorite Mexican recipes. She serves it over rice with a bowl of sour cream on the side.

1/2 cup raisins

4+ cups Turkey Stock (see p. 122)

4 dried ancho chilis

4 dried mulato chilis

1/3 cup pork fat, or peanut oil if fresh pork fat is unavailable

1 cup onions, chopped

2 tablespoons garlic, minced

1/4 teaspoon jalapeño pepper, minced*

1/3 pound tomatillos, peeled and finely chopped

3 tomatoes, peeled, deseeded, and finely chopped

1/2 cup almonds, blanched and toasted

1/4 cup pumpkin seeds, toasted

1 corn tortilla, shredded

2 pieces white bread, toasted and dry, crusts removed, and shredded

1 teaspoon ground cumin

1/4 teaspoon ground cloves

1/4 teaspoon ground cinnamon

2 ounces unsweetened chocolate

1-1/2 teaspoons salt

1-1/2 teaspoons sugar

2 cups cooked turkey meat, shredded into rather large pieces

Cilantro

Plump the raisins in a small amount of Turkey Stock and set aside. Put the 4 cups Turkey Stock on the stove to simmer.

Remove stems and seeds of the chilis, tear the chilis into small pieces, and put them into a saucepan. Pour 3 cups of the hot Turkey Stock over the chili pieces, bring to a boil, remove from the heat, cover, and let stand at least 1/2 hour.

In a heavy pot with a capacity of at least 4 quarts, melt the fat and sauté the onions, garlic, jalapeño pepper, and tomatillos until the onions are translucent. Add the tomatoes and simmer, stirring often, until the tomatoes are cooked and their liquid has evaporated. Turn off the heat and set aside.

In a food processor or blender, process the almonds and pumpkin seeds until they are very finely ground. Remove from the processor. Without washing the processor, add the chilis and the stock they have been soaking in and blend until the chilis are pureed.

Pour the chili/stock puree into the pot with the tomatillo sauce. Add the tortilla and toast pieces. Add the spices and the last cup of hot Turkey Stock and stir to mix.

In batches, process the sauce until the tortilla pieces are incorporated into the sauce, then return the sauce to the pot.

Add the chocolate, raisins and their liquid, and ground seeds and nuts; stir to mix, then simmer the sauce until the chocolate is melted, stirring from time to time. Add the salt, sugar, and turkey. Stir well. Adjust the seasonings and simmer a few minutes longer.

Serve over rice and garnish with freshly chopped cilantro.

Serves 6 to 8.

—————

*This makes a hot mole. Reduce the amount of jalapeño or omit it altogether, according to your tastes; the dish will still be quite piquant.

Stuffed Potato Gnocchi

Although several countries have developed their own forms of *gnocchi*—small, light, fluffy dumplings—the name *gnocchi* is Italian. The following recipe is made of light potato dough stuffed with a tasty turkey filling, topped with two rich sauces (one is plain melted butter), and garnished with freshly chopped Italian parsley. Make the Brown Onion Sauce (see p. 135) before you start and keep it warm in a double boiler or *bain-marie*.

FILLING

1/3 pound bacon, chopped
2/3 cup onions, minced
2 cups leftover cooked turkey meat,
  cut into small cubes
1/2 teaspoon marjoram
Salt
Pepper

In a hot, dry skillet, sauté the bacon. As soon as melted fat begins to accumulate, add the onions and sauté them until they are transparent. Add the turkey cubes and marjoram. Salt and pepper to taste, stir, and let cool thoroughly.

DOUGH

1 pound baking potatoes, cooked,
  peeled, cooled, and grated
1 cup flour
4 tablespoons instant Cream of
  Wheat
1/2 teaspoon salt
1/4 cup oil
1 egg

Place all ingredients in a large bowl and mix well with a wooden spoon or blend in an electric mixer with a dough hook. Do not overmix.

Turn onto a lightly floured board and form into a log approximately 2-1/2 inches in diameter. Wrap in plastic wrap and chill. When the dough is chilled and the filling is cool, proceed to make the *gnocchi*.

Slice the chilled dough log into 20 slices. Place one round slice in one hand and, with the fingers of the other hand, press and stretch the outer edges gently to enlarge the wheel slightly.

Then, still holding the dough in your palm, place a ball of filling in the center of the dough and bring the sides of the dough over the filling to cover it completely. Seal all the edges to cover the filling. The *gnocchi* will be football shaped.

Dust with flour as you would when making fresh pasta and lay the *gnocchi* carefully on a tray until ready for boiling.

Cook the stuffed *gnocchi* in boiling salted water just before serving. They are done when they float to the surface. Lift them out carefully with a slotted spoon and place them on a heated serving platter.

Melt 1/2-stick butter until it foams and pour over all the *gnocchi*. Spoon on the hot Brown Onion Sauce, sprinkle with chopped Italian parsley, and serve.

Serves 4.

Pastilla

Pastilla (spelled various ways) is an elaborate Moroccan pie with a many-layered filo crust dusted with confectioners' sugar and cinnamon. It has Berber, Arab, Persian, and Anadalusian influences, and is made, in its native land, with pigeons. Maggie Klein has adapted it to the dark meat of turkey—moist, flavorful meat that has a lot in common with pigeon meat, save the bones.

The recipe takes quite a while to prepare, but, with a salad, comprises a whole meal and is as elegant as it is delicious. Filo dough is available frozen at supermarkets.

2 turkey drumsticks
1 turkey thigh
3 cloves garlic, crushed
Salt
10 tablespoons butter (or more, depending on the weather)
1 onion, minced
1/2 cup parsley, chopped
Pinch pulverized saffron
1 tablespoon ginger, freshly grated
Ground cinnamon
1 teaspoon ground cumin
Red pepper flakes
3 cups Turkey Stock (see p. 122)
Zest of one lemon, grated
2 cups sliced almonds, toasted
Confectioners' sugar

8 eggs
1 pound filo dough, thawed
1/2 cup cilantro, chopped

Rub the turkey parts well with the garlic and a good shaking of salt. Melt 2 tablespoons of the butter in a large heavy pot and add the onion, parsley, saffron, ginger, 1/2 teaspoon ground cinnamon, cumin, and a good shake of red pepper flakes. Sauté until the onions are translucent.

Add the turkey pieces and Turkey Stock. Cover and simmer 1-1/2 hours or until the meat is very tender. Remove the turkey pieces from the liquid and let them cool. Remove the larger pieces of onion and turkey bits from the liquid with a slotted spoon and discard; skim the fat from the top. Boil the liquid and reduce it to 1-3/4 cups. Add the lemon zest.

Melt the rest (8 tablespoons) of the butter. Mix the almond slices in a bowl with 3 tablespoons confectioners' sugar and a sprinkling of powdered cinnamon. Drizzle 3 tablespoons melted butter over them and mix. Set aside.

Whisk the eggs together with a little salt until they are frothy. Bring the reduced turkey liquid to a rapid boil, and, stirring all the time, add the eggs to the liquid. Continue to cook and stir until the eggs have formed curds and are dry. (They will resemble scrambled eggs.) Remove from the heat immediately and transfer to a bowl to stop the cooking. Set aside.

Remove the skin from the turkey parts and shred the meat with your fingers, making sure the pieces are small. Put in a bowl, toss with a sprinkling of salt, and set aside.

Preheat the oven to 425° F.

Brush a large (12-inch by 3/4-inch) cake or pizza pan with melted butter. Lay out the filo dough under a moist towel to prevent the sheets from drying out. Replace the towel as you use the dough. Lay one sheet on the pan, with about half of it hanging over the side. Brush it quickly with butter. Continue overlapping the filo, going clockwise around the pan, brushing after each sheet is laid down. Put the sheets at the 12 o'clock, 2 o'clock, 4 o'clock positions and so forth until six sheets have been laid down. One by one, lay down four more sheets in the center of the pan, brushing after each is laid.

Fill the pie first with the almond mixture, then with the egg-curds (remove them from their bowl with a slotted spoon), then with the turkey meat, and top with cilantro, distributing each layer evenly. Fold the corners and ends of the filo over the filling in the reverse order in which the sheets were originally laid, brushing with melted butter as necessary.

Top the pie with four more sheets, laid, centered, over the pie and brushed with butter between each addition. Place a large baking sheet or round, flat pizza pan on the pie and flip the pie over onto the sheet. Remove the cake pan.

Add four more layers of filo, centered, brushing between additions. Put the cake pan back over the pie and flip again. Bring all the edges up and make a neat package, brushing with melted butter as necessary. With the rest of the filo sheets, place each sheet atop the pie, centered, brush with butter, and fold the edges up neatly until you have used all the dough.

Bake the pie for 15 minutes at 425° F, or until golden brown, then remove from the oven. Flip the pie onto the baking sheet and bake 10 minutes more or until the other side of the pie is golden brown. The pie should be served almond-side up.

Let the pie cool for up to half an hour before serving. Dust with plenty of confectioners' sugar and cinnamon; a lattice pattern is the most familiar and is quite pretty.

Serves 8.

Quiche

DOUGH

1-3/4 cups flour
Salt
1-1/2 sticks butter (6 ounces)
1 egg yolk
1/3 cup cold water

Mix the flour with a pinch of salt. Using a food processor—or pastry blender if you are making the dough by hand—cut the butter into the flour and salt until the mixture has the appearance of coarse meal. Beat the egg yolk and water together and add to the flour mixture. Process or stir with a wooden spoon until a dough forms. Gather into a ball, flatten, cover with plastic wrap, and set aside to rest for at least 30 minutes. (This will relax the gluten, make the dough easier to handle, and reduce shrinkage in baking.)

Preheat the oven to 400° F.

On a lightly floured board, roll the dough out in a circle. Gently fit the dough into the bottom of a 9-inch quiche pan with high sides. Trim the edges and wrap and refrigerate leftover dough for later use. Pierce the bottom with a fork in several places to prevent bubbling when baking. To help keep the bottom flat and the sides from falling, set a second pan into the crust or line the crust with foil or parchment and fill with dried beans. (The latter method is referred to as "baking blind.")

Prebake for 8 to 10 minutes at 400° F until the dough is set. This prevents the bottom from becoming soggy.

FILLING

2 tablespoons butter
1/2 cup onions, minced
1/2 parsley, minced
Meat and skin from one or more roasted drumsticks, shredded
1 cup grated hard cheese (dry Monterey Jack, Parmesan, or dry Swiss)
2 eggs, whole
2 egg yolks

1 cup milk
1/4 teaspoon cayenne pepper
1/2 teaspoon salt

Preheat the oven to 350° F.

In a skillet, melt the butter and sauté the onions with the parsley until the onions are transparent. Remove from the heat. In a bowl, combine the shredded turkey, 1/2 cup grated cheese, and onion mixture. Spread on the bottom of the partially baked pastry shell.

In a bowl, beat together the whole eggs, egg yolks, milk, pepper, and salt. Pour over the meat mixture in the shell. Sprinkle the remaining 1/2 cup grated cheese over all.

Bake at 350° F for 30 to 40 minutes or until the custard is firm. (When a knife inserted into the center comes out clean, the custard is set.) Cooking time is greatly determined by the shape of the pan and the material of which it is made.

For brunch or lunch, serve with tossed salad greens, cranberry relish, or a compote of fresh fruits.

Serves 6.

Turkey Pot Pie

CRUST

2 cups flour
1/2 teaspoon salt
1/2 pound butter (2 sticks)
1 egg
1/3 cup cold water

Mix the flour and salt. Using a food processor—or a pastry blender if you are making the dough by hand—cut the butter into the flour and salt until it has the appearance of coarse meal. Beat the egg and water together and add to the flour mixture. Process or stir with a wooden spoon until a dough forms. Gather into a ball, flatten a bit, wrap in plastic, and let rest for at least 30 minutes.

On a lightly floured board, roll out the dough in a circle the size of the top of a 1-1/2-quart baking casserole, about 1/4 inch thick.

FILLING

3-1/2 cups Turkey Velouté Sauce
  (see p. 131)
1/2 cup fresh mushrooms, sliced
1/4 cup onions, sliced
4 tablespoons butter
3/4 cup pea pods, fresh, blanched
1 tablespoon parsley, chopped
Meat from 2 roasted drumsticks,
  cubed (or add meat from roasted
  thighs and first joint of wings)
2 eggs, hard cooked and sliced
1 egg yolk
1 teaspoon water

Preheat the oven to 375° F.

Prepare the Turkey Velouté Sauce (see p. 131).

In a skillet, sauté the mushrooms and onions in the butter.

In a bowl, mix the pea pods, parsley, cubed turkey, and the mushroom and onion mixture. Place the mixture into a 1-1/2-quart baking casserole. Pour the Velouté Sauce over the mixture until it is covered. Layer the sliced eggs evenly over all.

Top with the circle of dough. Slash the dough in several places to allow steam to escape. Brush with an egg wash of 1 egg yolk blended with 1 teaspoon water.

Bake at 375° F for 25 minutes or until the crust is golden brown and the turkey mixture is hot.

A dessert of fresh fruit and cheese will complement this dish very nicely.

Serves 6 to 8 for lunch.

Turkey Cosenza

Maggie Klein uses dark turkey meat in her version of the Italian sausage known as *cosenza*—a spicy sausage which usually has a stubby shape. Do not overprocess the meat as it will lose its characteristic texture.

40 inches sausage casing
1-1/2 pounds dark turkey meat, well trimmed and chopped
1/2 pound pork back fat, chopped
3 ounces red wine
1 tablespoon dried red pepper flakes

6 cloves garlic, crushed
2 teaspoons ground coriander seeds
2 teaspoons salt

Rinse the salt off the sausage casing, soak in water, and put aside.

Put the meat and fat in a processor and process until just mixed. Add the wine, pepper, garlic, coriander, and salt and process again until just mixed. Proceed, using the instructions for making *boudin blanc* (p. 96).

Makes 10 sausages.

Turkey in Pancetta en Brochette

These little rolls, served right from the broiler, make either an excellent hors d'oeuvre or a delightful main course.

*2 turkey thighs, uncooked, boned
(see p. 56), and skinned*
Salt
2 cloves garlic, minced
3 tablespoons olive oil
*16 strips pancetta (Italian bacon) at
least 4 inches long*
16 or more fresh sage or basil leaves
4 skewers

Bone the turkey thighs (see p. 56) and remove the skin. (Save the bones and skin for the stock pot.) Cut the thigh meat into eight equal-sized pieces and salt lightly.

In a small bowl, mix the garlic with the olive oil. Roll the pieces of turkey meat in it to coat.

Arrange the pancetta strips side by side on a cutting board. Place one (or two, if the leaves are tiny) of the herb leaves on one end of the pancetta. Place a turkey piece on the leaf and, starting at the end with the turkey meat, roll as tightly as possible.

Oil the skewers lightly and impale four rolls on each skewer. (Oiling the skewers will enable you to slide the cooked rolls easily onto a dish when they are served.) Make sure you pierce the end of each pancetta slice so it will not unwind.

Broil on the broiling rack for about 5 minutes on each side until the pancetta is brown and crisp.

Remove from the broiler and let rest for 2 minutes to allow for recirculation of the juices. Slide the meat rolls off the skewer with the prongs of your cooking fork, scraping the rolls off with one smooth motion onto the plate.

Serves 4.

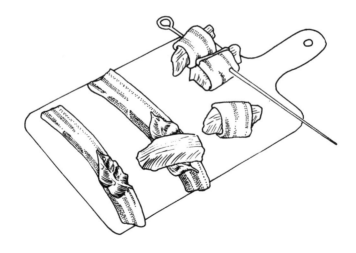

Paprikash

Paprikash is a traditional Hungarian dish. The half cup of good Hungarian paprika called for in this recipe gives a very distinctive flavor and texture. Reduced preparation time is a short 30 minutes. The technique of cooking the meat in the already pureed and starchless sauce eliminates unnecessary handling and reduces the danger of scorching.

2 cups Turkey Stock (see p. 122)
2 turkey thighs, uncooked, boned (see p. 56), and skinned
Salt
1/4 cup oil
2 cups onions, coarsely chopped
3 large cloves garlic, crushed
2 ounces tomato paste (one-third small can)
1 cup sour cream
2 tablespoons flour
1/2 cup Hungarian paprika
Noodles or rice

Prepare the Turkey Stock and set aside.

Bone the turkey thighs and remove the skin. Trim the meat well and cut into 1-inch cubes. Salt lightly. Set aside.

In a skillet, heat the oil and sauté the onions and garlic to a light brown. Add 1/2 cup of the Turkey Stock and bring to a boil. Allow to cool slightly. Pour into a food processor or blender and puree.

Place the resulting puree into a saucepan, add the turkey cubes, the tomato paste, and the remaining cup of Turkey Stock. Bring to a boil and then lower the heat to simmer until the meat is *al dente*, approximately 25 minutes.

When the meat is ready, whip the sour cream, flour, and paprika together, blending well. Pour over the meat and liquid in the saucepan, mix well, and bring to a full boil for 30 seconds. Serve at once. Bulgur, couscous, or dumplings are nice accompaniments.

Serves 4.

★ ★

Pasta with Ginger and Peppers

Maggie Klein developed this recipe for a first-course pasta dish, characterized by the refreshing flavors of lemon and ginger. Make sure all the ingredients that go into the dish are cut as thin as possible so they complement the very thin pasta.

Olive oil

2 red bell peppers, deseeded and julienned very thin

2 tablespoons fresh ginger, grated

2 bunches green onions, cut lengthwise very thin

4 cloves garlic, crushed

Zest of one lemon, grated

1 cup cooked turkey leftovers, shredded into long, thin pieces

Salt

1 pound capellini, Japanese somen, or other fine pasta

In 4 tablespoons olive oil, sauté the pepper strips, ginger, onions, and garlic in a large, heavy casserole. When the peppers are limp, add the lemon and turkey, sprinkle with salt, and mix.

In a large pot, boil plenty of water and salt it. When it is boiling rapidly, add the pasta all at once, stir immediately, and cook until just *al dente*. (It shouldn't take more than a minute, depending on the width of the pasta.) Pour immediately into a colander and rinse with warm water. After the pasta has drained, put it next to the stove and turn the heat on under the casserole of peppers. Add the pasta a little at a time, alternating with a drizzle of olive oil, and mix after each addition. (With such fine pasta it is difficult to toss it all at once and distribute the seasoning and vegetables.) Salt to taste. Do not skimp on olive oil.

Serves 6 as a first course.

★ ★

Turkey Thighs Grand Veneur

This interesting recipe is a "hunter-style" dish. It calls for the unusual combination of spicy tomato sauce, sour cream, and cranberries. Make sure the skillet you use can be transferred to the oven (that its handles are neither plastic nor composition).

2 boned (see p. 56), larded (see p. 64) thighs
Salt
2 tablespoons peanut oil
3 cloves garlic, mashed and minced very fine, almost to a paste
1/2 cup onions, minced
2 tablespoons pork fat or bacon
1 cup dry red wine
1 cup Spicy Tomato Sauce (see p. 134)
1/2 cup sour cream combined with 1 tablespoon flour
1/2 cup whole cranberry sauce

Preheat the oven to 400° F.

Place the larded, salted thighs in a well-oiled, 10-inch skillet. Put the skillet into a 400° F oven and roast for 15 minutes. Sauté the garlic and onions in the pork fat and set aside.

When the thighs are roasted, remove them from the skillet. Let them recirculate for 10 minutes at room temperature, then place in a warming oven. Discard the fat from the skillet; deglaze the drippings in the skillet on top of the stove with the red wine, scraping the sides and bottom well and allowing the liquid to cook and reduce.

Add the sautéed onions and the Spicy Tomato Sauce, stir, and simmer for 3 to 4 minutes. Add the sour cream and flour mixture and blend well. Strain into a clean pan. Add the cranberries, bring to a boil, adjust for salt, and keep warm.

Slice the roasted thighs, arrange them on a platter, and cover lightly with the sauce.

Serves 6.

Mesquite-Broiled Roquefort Patties

The melted Roquefort cheese on these turkey patties, together with the pungent thinly sliced red onion, make a sophisticated version of the classic barbecued hamburger.

6 cups turkey meat, boneless and skinless (may be all dark or mixed, with trimmings from other cuts)
1 egg
1 teaspoon salt
1 teaspoon ground sage
White pepper
1/3 cup half-and-half cream, well chilled
1/4 pound ripe, imported Roquefort cheese
1/2 stick unsalted butter
Butter lettuce
1 large red onion
1/2 bunch watercress, washed and picked clean
French bread, with patty-sized circumference

Cut the turkey meat into very small pieces, removing all the skin and ligaments. Refrigerate until quite well chilled. Chop in the processor for 10 seconds, add the egg and the salt, sage, and pepper to taste, and process for 5 seconds more.

Add the cream and blend quickly. Do not allow the meat to lose its texture.

Divide the meat mixture into eight patties and refrigerate, well wrapped in plastic wrap.

Blend the Roquefort and the butter into a paste. Wash and select eight uniform lettuce leaves from the tender part of the head; pat dry. Slice eight thin rounds from the middle of the onion.

Place the meat over hot mesquite charcoals. While the meat broils on the grill to medium well, toast eight slices of French bread and spread generously with the Roquefort butter. Place a lettuce leaf on each piece and arrange watercress sprigs on the lettuce.

Top with the juicy patty, garnish with an onion slice, and serve at once as an open-face sandwich.

Serves 8.

Turkey Curry

The taste of this dish will depend greatly on the quality of the curry. I recommend using imported Indian curry, or, better yet, making your own (see p. 133); you will have a much superior dish to one prepared with domestic curry.

Generally, turkey wings from a 22- to 24-pound turkey are large enough to allow one per serving. However, you must use your own judgment concerning the appetites of your diners.

1 cup Curry Sauce (see p. 133)
Turkey Stock (see p. 122)
Salt
4 turkey wings, uncooked (center section with 2 bones)

Curry powder
2 ounces butter
1/2 cup heavy cream
Prepare the Curry Sauce and the Turkey Stock and set aside.

115

Salt the wings lightly and rub in the curry powder. Melt the butter in a skillet. As soon as the butter foams, sauté the turkey wings over a medium heat quickly. Turn them once; do not brown.

Add enough Turkey Stock to barely cover. Bring to a simmer, cover, and simmer until tender—30 minutes or more.

When the wings are tender, transfer them to a warm platter. Add the curry sauce and cream to the liquid in the pot. Bring to a boil and reduce to a smooth sauce.

Serve wings hot on a bed of plain rice, cover with sauce, and garnish with chutney. Other rice combinations, such as a mild risotto or oriental-type fried rice, are equally compatible.

Serves 4.

Turkey Wings Cacciatore

Cacciatore is the Italian word for *hunter*, or *hunter-style*.

Read this recipe carefully before starting, visualizing the steps. At first it may seem as if you are doing a great deal of transferring, but the separation of the ingredients in the cooking is very important. Wings have a longer cooking time than the vegetables, so by cooking them separately, you will preserve all the individual flavors of the ingredients. The result is a multi-flavored, fresh tasting, delicious dish.

1/2 cup Turkey Stock (see p. 122)
Salt
4 turkey wings, uncooked (center section with 2 bones)
Pepper
Flour
4 tablespoons olive oil
1/2 cup onions, thinly sliced
3 cloves garlic, minced
1/2 cup dry white wine
1/2 teaspoon dried basil
1 cup tomatoes, peeled, deseeded, and diced
1/2 bell pepper, julienne sliced
1/2 cup celery, sliced
1/2 cup mushrooms, sliced

Prepare the Turkey Stock and set aside.

Salt the turkey wings lightly and grind some fresh black pepper over them if you wish. Roll in flour. In a skillet, heat 2 tablespoons of the olive oil and sauté the wings, turning once. Do not brown. Set aside the skillet and wings.

Using a saucepan large enough to later accommodate the wings, heat the remaining 2 tablespoons of olive oil and sauté the onions and the garlic until the onions are transparent but not browned.

Deglaze with the wine and the stock. Sprinkle in the basil and transfer the sautéed wings to this pan. Cover with a tight-fitting lid and simmer for 20 minutes.

Add the tomatoes and leave the cover off so they will reduce while cooking over a low heat.

Into the skillet in which the wings were originally sautéed and which still has some oil in it, place the bell pepper and celery and sauté over a high heat. Add more olive oil if necessary. When the vegetables start to brown, add the mushrooms, stir gently, and sauté briefly. Remove from the heat.

When the wings are tender, remove them from their skillet and place them on a heated serving platter. Then combine the mixtures from the two pans and spoon the sauce over the wings. Serve hot.

Italian polenta (cornmeal) or gnocchi Romano (made with farina or cream of wheat) makes a fine companion dish.

Serves 4.

STOCK AND SOUPS

T urkey stock is the liquid that results from the simmering of bones, gristle, skin, giblets, herbs, spices, and vegetables. (The liver should never be used in stock as it tends to be bitter.) Unlike broth, in which edible portions of meat are cooked sectioning, disjointing, or dividing the turkey. A high-sided stock pot with a lid is essential. Be sure that it is large enough to hold all the ingredients and still provide enough space so the stock does not boil over.

The bones or carcass should be

> *"Some of the new cooks are more interested in the fashion business than in the science of cuisine."* **KW**

in liquid, the stocks are strained and the trimmings discarded (with the possible exception of the giblets, which can be diced and used in gravy). The resulting flavorful liquid makes a rich base for soups, gravies, and sauces.

The making of stock is an almost automatic companion activity to broken up to fit in the pot and be completely covered with cold water. The use of cold water is important as it will leach or extract the most nutrients and flavor from the ingredients in the stock.

Turkey Stock

*Carcass and other bones removed
from the turkey*

*Neck, gizzard, and heart from the
turkey*

5 medium carrots, scrubbed

*6 stalks of celery (the heavy, dark,
outside stalks and some leaves)*

*3 medium onions, peeled and stud-
ded with 2 or 3 whole cloves each*

3 bay leaves

1 tablespoon pickling spice

Optional:

Parsley stems

Parsnips

Leeks or green onions

1 or 2 fresh tomatoes, quartered

Place all the ingredients in a stock pot that will accommodate them comfortably when the ingredients are covered with cold water. Bring to a boil, then reduce the heat to simmering for at least 4 hours. (See p. 25) The lid should be placed ajar during this period to hasten the heating.

It is important that the water level be maintained to cover the bones while simmering. The addition of boiling water may be necessary if the stock begins to evaporate or reduce. Add only very hot water to avoid cooling the stock. It should continue to simmer uninterrupted.

Do not salt at this time. Proper seasoning will take place when the stock is used in a particular dish.

Strain the stock, cool, cover, and refrigerate. The next day, remove the congealed fat which has risen to the surface and discard it. The stock is now ready for use immediately or it should be refrigerated or frozen for later use.

Sherried Consommé

Serve this clear consommé piping hot in bouillon cups for a distinctive and elegant first course.

*2-1/2 quarts Turkey Stock, defatted
    (see p. 122)*
Bones, left over after *roasting and
    removing the meat*
*Skin from roasted turkey, left over
    after carving*
1 large onion
4 stalks celery
1 parsnip
1 large carrot
1/2 bunch parsley (including stems)
1 teaspoon salt
1 teaspoon basil
1 teaspoon marjoram
1/2 teaspoon ground cardamom
3 egg whites and their shells
Dry sherry

Use the prepared Turkey Stock in which to boil the already roasted bones and skin. Simmer for 2 hours. The additional simmering will reinforce the flavor of the stock.

Because one of the characteristics of good consommé is a clean and sparkling appearance, strain the new stock to make it as clear as possible, then cool and defat it. Two quarts of the resulting cold stock are further clarified as follows.

Chop coarsely with a knife and place the onion, celery, parsnip, carrot, and parsley in a food processor. Process the mixture until it is finely chopped. Add the salt, basil, marjoram, cardamom, 1 cup cold defatted stock, and egg whites and shells. Continue to process until blended.

In a large pot, mix the contents of the processor with the rest of the cold, defatted stock. Stir well to keep the egg whites well distributed and bring slowly to a simmer. As soon as foam collects on the surface, stop stirring and allow the simmering to continue undisturbed. This will enable the vegetables and egg whites to coagulate into a solid mass and absorb the bits of material that cloud the liquid.

Remove from the heat and carefully strain through a filter in a sieve or china cap.

Measure the resulting consommé so you can determine how much dry sherry to add just before serving. The proper proportion is 1 cup consommé to 1 scant tablespoon sherry.

Salt to taste after the sherry has been added.

Sopa de Guajolote
con Frijoles

This hearty soup (which, translated from Spanish, means simply *turkey soup with beans)* makes a wonderful one-dish meal which would be especially welcome on a cold winter's day. It is so thick it is almost a turkey chili; add stock for a soup consistency. The flavor improves if made in advance. Serve with hot buttered cornbread.

7 cups Turkey Stock (see p. 122), defatted

1-1/2 cups dried pinto beans, washed
1 cup potatoes, peeled and diced

1/2 cup oil

3 cloves garlic, minced

1/2 cup onions, minced

1/2 cup celery, minced

*1 fresh red pepper (hot or mild),
minced*

*1 fresh yellow pepper (hot or mild),
minced*

1 tablespoon cumin, ground

3 tablespoons chili powder

1/2 teaspoon thyme

*1-1/2 cups tomatoes, peeled,
deseeded, and diced*

*Turkey meat from stock bones (neck,
carcass, etc.) or any other cooked
leftover turkey meat, coarsely
chopped*

Salt

Cilantro

Prepare the Turkey Stock.

Soak the washed beans in 3-1/2 cups cold Turkey Stock over night. The next day, add the remaining stock, bring to a boil, then reduce the heat and let simmer, stirring from time to time to prevent sticking.

After the beans have simmered for 1 hour, add the potatoes and continue to cook until the beans and potatoes are tender.

In a skillet, heat the oil and add the garlic, onions, celery, and peppers. Sauté until the onions are transparent. Stir in the spices and cook briefly. Then stir the mixture into the soup. Use a large wire whisk to blend, mashing some of the beans and potatoes as you do so. Bring to a boil, reduce the heat, and simmer for 3 minutes.

Add the diced tomatoes and the chopped turkey. Bring back to a boil; salt to taste before serving. Sprinkle with freshly chopped cilantro.

Serves 8.

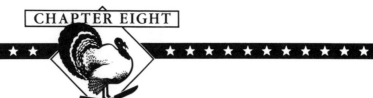

GRAVY AND SAUCES

★ ★

Turkey gravy consists of the roast's drippings diluted with a little turkey stock and very lightly thickened. Turkey gravy should not look like a fatless, thin consommé; it should be a smooth, pale brown, or complement a dish, but they are noticeably thicker than gravies. Unlike gravy, which must be made from the drippings of the meat with which it is used, sauces do not always contain the same meat flavor.

"It's a good attitude to taste often." KW

---

light syrup. Good gravy is a by-product of roasted meat and can be obtained only by careful roasting and browning (not burning). The gravy is a browned mixture of fat, liquid, and *mirepoix* (see p. 24). Gravy must be strained and is used in much the same manner as sauce.

Sauces are also rich, smoothly thickened liquids used to enhance

Plan to prepare 1/3 cup of gravy or sauce per serving of each dish. Most leftover sauces freeze well.

Roast Turkey Gravy

5 cups Turkey Stock (see p. 122), hot
1/2 cup onions, roughly cubed
1/2 cup celery, roughly cubed
1/2 cup carrots, roughly cubed
8 tablespoons flour
1 teaspoon paprika
Salt

Prepare the Turkey Stock.

Remove the turkey parts you have roasted from the pan and place the pan—with all the drippings—on the stove top. Use two burners if necessary. Add the onions, celery, and carrots (the *mirepoix*) and stir well.

Cook and reduce the drippings over a low heat until the remaining fat is clear.

Drain off all the fat and measure 5 table-spoons of it into a small skillet and set aside.

To the roasting pan, add the hot Turkey Stock, stirring constantly. Bring to a boil and reduce to simmering.

Over a medium heat in the small skillet with the fat, blend in the flour and the paprika, making a smooth paste (roux). Cook for 1 minute, cool a little, and add to the simmering stock in the roasting pan. Scrape gently from the bottom and walls of the pan to incorporate all the flavorful drippings and particles. Cook for at least 10 minutes until the gravy is thickened to the desired consistency. Add more stock as needed to thin, or cook longer to reduce.

Strain through a fine sieve or china cap. Correct salt or other seasoning and keep warm over hot water in a *bain-marie* or double boiler.

Makes 1 quart of gravy. Freezes well.

Turkey Velouté Sauce

Although this sauce is made with Turkey Stock, it complements veal and chicken dishes well.

5 cups Turkey Stock (see p. 122), hot
2 tablespoons onion, minced
4 tablespoons oil or 5 tablespoons
  butter
8 tablespoons flour
Salt

Prepare the Turkey Stock.

In a sauce pan, sauté the onions in the oil or butter until the foam subsides. Do not brown. Stir in the flour, blending smoothly with a flexible wire whisk to prevent lumping.

Remove the pan from the heat and cool for several minutes.

Add the hot Turkey Stock all at once, blending gently with the whisk to keep the sauce smooth. Bring to a full boil. Reduce the heat and allow to simmer at least 10 minutes. Strain through a fine sieve or china cap.

Correct the seasoning and keep warm over hot water in a *bain-marie* or double boiler.

Makes approximately 4 cups of sauce. Freezes well.

Tomates Concassées Sauce

1 cup Turkey Velouté Sauce
  (see p. 131), hot
2 tablespoons olive oil
1 large clove garlic, peeled and
  crushed
2 tablespoons onion, grated
2 large tomatoes, peeled, deseeded,
  and diced
Salt
Sugar
Dried basil

Prepare the Turkey Velouté Sauce and set aside.

In a medium-sized skillet, heat the olive oil and sauté the crushed garlic to impart flavor to the oil. Remove and discard the garlic.

Place the grated onion in the garlicked oil and sauté briefly. Add the diced tomatoes, season with salt, a dash of sugar, and a sprinkling of dried basil. Add the hot Turkey Velouté Sauce and bring to a boil.

Generally, the longer a sauce is cooked, the more reduced and thick it becomes. This sauce, however, becomes more watery the longer it cooks because of the liquid in the fresh tomatoes. Therefore, do not prolong cooking after the sauce reaches a full boil.

Because fresh tomatoes will loose texture, this sauce does not freeze well and should be made fresh for each use.

Makes 2 cups.

Curry Sauce

Imported Indian curry is vastly superior to and much more tasty than domestic varieties. Every effort should be made to use it—or make your own curry.* If you do make your own curry, experiment according to your preference for hot or mild flavors.

3 cups Turkey Stock (see p. 122), hot
3 ounces butter
1/2 cup onion, very finely minced
4 cloves garlic, peeled and crushed
3 tablespoons curry powder*
1 cup potato, peeled and cut into
  small cubes
Salt

Prepare the Turkey Stock and set aside.

In a saucepan, melt the butter and sauté the onion and garlic. Add the curry powder and blend well.

Pour in the hot Turkey Stock all at once and stir with a wire whisk. Blend until smooth. Add the potatoes and bring to a boil; reduce the heat and simmer for about 10 minutes, or until the potatoes are soft. Mash to thicken the sauce as desired. Add salt to taste.

Makes about 2 cups of sauce. Freezes well.

———————

*Buy imported Indian curry or make your own curry with the following proportions of ground spices: 2-1/2 teaspoons turmeric, 2 teaspoons coriander, 1-1/2 teaspoons cumin, 1 teaspoon ginger, 1/2 teaspoon cardamom, 1/2 teaspoon clove, 1/2 teaspoon fenugreek, 1/2 teaspoon allspice, 1/2 teaspoon nutmeg, 1/4 teaspoon cayenne pepper, 1/4 teaspoon dill weed, 1/4 teaspoon cinnamon.

Spicy Tomato Sauce

The spicy flavor of this sauce comes from the jalapeño pepper and coriander. The proportions of these ingredients can be adjusted to suit your own taste.

6 cups Turkey Stock (see p. 122), hot

6 ounces butter

1/4 cup onion, finely minced

1/4 cup cilantro, finely minced

6 ounces tomato paste

1 small jalapeño pepper, dried and crumbled

White pepper

Salt

Sugar

1 teaspoon coriander, ground

Prepare the Turkey Stock and set aside.

In a saucepan, melt the butter. Add the onions and cilantro and sauté until the onions are transparent but not browned. Blend in the Turkey Stock, tomato paste, and dried pepper. Add the white pepper, salt, dash of sugar, and coriander. Reduce over a high heat until the liquid is saucelike.

Makes about 5 cups of sauce. Freezes well.

Brown Onion Sauce

Besides being the sauce for the Stuffed Potato Gnocchi on page 100, this sauce will complement almost any meat dish. It is an onion lover's delight.

2 cups onions, cut into small cubes
1 stick butter
2 cloves garlic, minced
2 tablespoons tomato paste
1/2 cup flour
5 cups Turkey Stock (p. 122), hot
1/2 teaspoon oregano
Salt

In a saucepan, sauté the onions in the melted butter. Add the garlic and tomato paste and continue to sauté until the tomato caramelizes.

Remove the pan from the heat, stir in the flour, and blend into a paste. Add 3 cups of the hot Turkey Stock and stir until smooth.

Stir in the remaining hot stock, blend well, and bring to a boil. Add the oregano.

Lower the heat and simmer at least 5 minutes. Check for texture. If it is too thin, bring to a vigorous boil and stir constantly for another 3 to 4 minutes to reduce.

Salt to taste.

STUFFINGS

Perhaps the original stuffings were the creations of thrifty cooks who wanted to extend the number of meat servings at a meal and to use up stale bread and leftover rice and grains that might otherwise have the hours of cooking time required to roast a large stuffed turkey in the traditional manner.

Teamed with the rib cage, backbones, and hip bones of the bird, this mass presents a solid wall that takes heat rays hours to penetrate

---

"Doctors know little about nutrition; nutritionists know little about cooking." **KW**

---

been thrown out. Now, however, poultry and stuffing are inseparable partners. To serve roast turkey without stuffing could incite a family riot and endanger a great tradition.

Unfortunately it is this great, solid mass of flavorful starch, packed densely into the belly of the turkey, that is partly responsible for and cook (roast) into a safe and edible form.

Now, with the new thermodynamic approach—regardless of which parts of the turkey are served—rich, moist, flavorful stuffing can be prepared as a side dish without a long roasting time. Turkey skin from any part of the turkey that is not being used (the neck

flap, the back, or the breast, for example) or bacon strips can be used as a topping or wrapping for the stuffing. Herbs, spices, vegetables, turkey stock, and turkey gravy are used for seasoning. Even though the stuffing is cooked separately from the bird, the turkey flavor is still there. Good stuffing recipes are infinite; here are two of my favorites.

Bread and Herb Stuffing

You will find that the melting fat from the skin imparts a wonderful turkey flavor to this stuffing. Serve it right from the baking pan at the table and eliminate all the messiness of spooning it out from the bird. The separate pan also enables you to roast in a much shorter time and makes it easier to keep leftovers safely. (Stuffing that remains inside the turkey always presents a worry because the warm, dark environment is an ideal place for bacteria to develop.)

Stale French bread with all the crusts trimmed is the best bread for this stuffing.

6 cups bread cubes
1/4 pound (1 stick) + 2 tablespoons
 butter
1/2 cup onions, minced

1/2 cup green onions, thinly sliced
 (use part of tops also)
1/2 cup cilantro, minced (if not
 available, use parsley)

2 tablespoons fresh thyme
1 teaspoon nutmeg
1 egg
2 egg yolks
1 cup Turkey Stock (see p. 122)
Turkey skin, uncooked
Salt

Preheat the oven to 375° to 400° F.

In a large skillet, make crisp croutons by frying the bread cubes in 1/4 pound butter. Remove the croutons from the skillet and set aside. Add 2 tablespoons butter to the skillet and sauté the onions and herbs.

In a large bowl, beat the egg, egg yolks, and Turkey Stock. Then add the onion and herb mixture. Mix well and add the croutons. Allow to rest, stirring occasionally so the croutons will absorb all the liquid.

Pack the crouton mixture into a buttered, fireproof baking pan, smoothing the top. Cover with the pieces of turkey skin sprinkled with salt. Bake at 375 to 400° F until the skin is crisp.

The stuffing is done when a knife or toothpick inserted into the center of the stuffing comes out clean.

Bread with Mushroom and Ham Stuffing

This stuffing is designed to use up leftovers speedily, with no sautéeing and no elaborate preparation. You can use leftover baked ham or fried bacon. The flavoring in this stuffing is the familiar sage.

8 cups stale whole wheat bread

1-1/2 cups ham, minced (or leftover fried bacon)

1/2 cup onions, minced

1-1/2 cups mushrooms, sliced

1/2 cup parsley, minced

1 tablespoon dried sage

2 eggs

1-1/2 cups milk

Salt

Butter

Raw, lean bacon, sliced

Preheat the oven to 350° F.

Tear the bread into small pieces and mix it in a bowl with the ham, onions, mushrooms, parsley, and sage.

In another bowl, beat the eggs with the milk. Pour the egg and milk mixture over the bread, combine well, and allow to stand for 5 minutes while the bread absorbs the liquid. Stir occasionally and salt to taste.

Pack the stuffing into a buttered, fireproof baking pan, smoothing the top. Cover with a layer of bacon slices and bake at 350° F until the bacon topping is crisp and a knife inserted into the center of the stuffing comes out clean.

This stuffing can be served at the table right from the baking pan. It also freezes well.

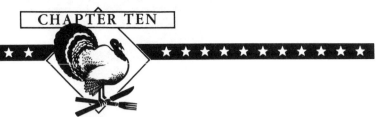
THE COLD BUFFET

The cold buffet has become common—almost traditional—fare in American cuisine. It is particularly helpful when there are many guests to be fed and the host or hostess would rather mingle with the crowd than be cooking over a hot stove.

Because of its high yield, delicious taste, and versatility, turkey lends itself beautifully to the cold buffet. It can be served simply sliced or used as an ingredient in a variety of recipes. For the artistic cook, it can be prepared as a showpiece *en belle vue.* No matter how it is utilized, turkey adds much to the attractiveness and succulence of the buffet, without great expense.

"Do you want a clean kitchen or do you want good turkey?" **KW**

Galantine

The key to a smooth and tasty galantine is using very chilled or partially frozen ingredients. This recipe makes two elegant turkey galantines which may be served as an hors d'oeuvre or as the main course of a dinner.

2 cups Turkey Stock (see p. 122),
* defatted and well chilled or*
* partially frozen*
1 turkey breast, uncooked, boned
* (see p. 59), and skinned (see p. 64)*
1 turkey thigh, uncooked, boned (see
* p. 56), skinned, coarsely chopped,*
* and well chilled*
Skin from breast and thighs
Salt
White pepper
1/2 teaspoon nutmeg
1/2 teaspoon ground ginger
4 egg whites, well chilled or
* partially frozen*

Prepare the Turkey Stock, breast (with the upper wing joint removed), and thigh, and set aside.

Preheat the oven to 325° F.

Oil two standard meatloaf pans (approximately 9 inches by 5 inches by 3 inches) and line them with raw turkey skin, allowing the pieces to hang over the sides several inches.

Cut the breast across into eight thick slices. Pound lightly to flatten and sprinkle with salt and white pepper. Line the two long sides and the bottoms of the pans, laying three slices of breast on top of the skin. Reserve the last slices.

Puree the chilled dark meat and all the trimmings left from the breast in a food processor until a fine paste is formed. Add salt, white pepper, nutmeg, ginger, and the partially frozen egg whites. Continue to process for 1 minute more to make an even smoother mass.

Add the partially frozen Turkey Stock while continuing to blend. When the mixture is well blended, mound it into the prepared pans, smoothing the tops. Cover with the reserved slices of breast. Bring the ends of the skin up, overlapping to cover the tops.

Place the molds into larger pans half filled with boiling water. This will create a water bath to control the slow baking of the galantines. Bake at 325° F until the internal temperature of the molds registers 138° F. Start checking after 1-1/4 hours. Any further cooking will change your galantines to dry meatloaves.

Remove the galantine pans from the water pans, place a small flat tray or board directly on top of each galantine, and weight (with some canned goods, perhaps) while they cool. The weights must not exceed 1-1/2 pounds. Refrigerate the galantines, with the weights, at least 12 hours.

Unmold the galantines by running the tip of a paring knife around the sides, and setting the bottom of the pans into very hot water to melt the fat and meat gelatins and release the bases. Turn the galantines out, rinse them with cold water, and place them on a serving platter.

Slice and garnish.

Pasta Salad with Turkey

As a buffet dish, this salad supplies a sophisticated but hearty starch. Use your favorite small pasta—*semini di melo, conchiglie,* or *tortiglioni,* for example.

Salt

1/2 green bell pepper, julienne sliced

1/2 red bell pepper, julienne sliced

1/2 cup red or Maui onions, thinly sliced

8 ounces pasta

2 cups cooked turkey, shredded

1 to 1-1/2 cups homemade mayonnaise, made at a ratio of 2:1 peanut to olive oil

Romaine lettuce

1/4 pound sliced Italian salami, julienne sliced

California dry-cured olives

Parsley

In separate bowls, salt the peppers and onions liberally. Cover with weighted plates and allow the salt to draw moisture while you cook the pasta.

In a large pot with an ample amount of boiling salted water, cook the pasta until it is *al dente.* Drain, rinse with cold water, and drain again thoroughly.

Squeeze the peppers and the onions by hand to remove as much liquid as possible. Toss them in a large bowl with the pasta, turkey, and enough mayonnaise to moisten. Mound the salad into a glass bowl lined with romaine spears. Sprinkle with the salami and garnish with the olives and parsley.

Serves 6.

Turkey and Apple Salad Grand Marnier

2 oranges

1 lemon

2 apples, firm and somewhat tart

2 egg yolks

3/4 cup peanut oil

Meat from 1 roasted drumstick, cooled and cut into small cubes

2 stalks tender celery, minced

Grand Marnier liqueur

Salt

Pepper

Butter lettuce, washed and dried

Slivered almonds, toasted

Nicoise olives

Remove and reserve the zest from the oranges and the lemon. Peel, core, and cut the apples into small cubes. Toss them in a bowl with the juice from the lemon and one orange so the apples will not turn brown. Set aside.

Peel the other orange, slice crosswise, and set aside for a garnish.

Place the egg yolks in a food processor or blender. Drain the citrus juices from the bowl of apples and add 3 tablespoons of the juice to the yolks. Turn on the processor. As the yolks are being processed, pour in the oil *very slowly* to make a mayonnaise. If you add the oil too fast, the emulsion will not be firm. Salt to taste.

In a mixing bowl, combine the apple cubes, turkey, celery, citrus zests, and a splash of Grand Marnier. Add the salt and pepper to taste.

Add enough of the mayonnaise to coat ingredients well. Cover and allow the flavors to blend for at least 1 hour. Serve the salad within 4 hours.

To serve in individual portions, fill butter lettuce "cups" with the salad. Sprinkle with the toasted almonds, and garnish with an orange slice topped with two or three small olives.

★ ★

Smoked Turkey Breast

For those who are especially fond of smoke-cooking, smoked turkey breast can be the ultimate in elegance.

Prepare a boned turkey breast (p. 59) with the wing removed. Lard the breast if you like (p. 64). Salt the breast well and smoke-cook it in a kettle-type barbecue or on a barbecue with a smoking attachment. The most popular woods for smoking are hickory, mesquite, and alder wood. Each adds its own distinctive flavor.

Cook the breast until the internal temperature registers 138° F. The length of time will vary between 2 and 3 hours depending on the heat of the coals and the thickness of the meat.

When the breast is cooked, cool and store it at least 3 to 4 days in an airtight wrap in the refrigerator. Slice thin and serve cold.

★ ★

Barbecued Cured Breast

The curing salt required for this recipe is available at most gourmet cooking shops and grocery stores, and some butchers carry it. This spicy, smoky cut, properly wrapped and refrigerated, will keep fresh up to 10 days.

1 boneless turkey breast (see p. 59), skin on but wing completely removed

1 ounce curing salt mix
1/2 teaspoon ground coriander
1/2 teaspoon allspice

1/2 teaspoon pepper
8 juniper berries, crushed
1 whole clove, crushed
1 bay leaf
Peanut oil

Wash the breast and drain but do not dry. Rub in all the salt and the spices.

Place the breast in a narrow, non-oxydizing container (glass, china, or stainless steel), cover the meat with plastic wrap, and weight it with 3 to 4 pounds canned goods or the like. Distribute the weight evenly over the meat. Keep well refrigerated for 2 days.

After 2 days, turn the meat, rewrap, and reweight (again equalizing the weight over the entire piece of meat). Refrigerate again for 2 days. Enough liquid should develop to cover the meat.

Repeat this procedure for a total of 8 days but not more than 2 weeks for complete curing.

When you are ready to cook the breast, remove it from the brine and rinse it in lukewarm water. Drain well. Oil all sides thoroughly and cook in a barbecue over a low heat for about 1 hour to an internal temperature of 138° F. Cool, wrap, and refrigerate the meat.

Serve thinly sliced.

Garnished Turkey Breast

This preparation is a dramatic and extremely satisfying creation for any cook. It is formally called "Turkey en Belle Vue." It presents the turkey in a delightful and unusual manner which serves as the focal point for a buffet.

2 larded turkey breasts (halves) (see Chapter 4), roasted and completely cooled

8 cups Turkey Potato Salad (see p. 153)

Hard-cooked eggs, sliced

Tomatoes

Assorted brine-cured olives (Kalamatas, for example)

Capers

Italian parsley, watercress, or cilantro

Prepare the breasts and 8 cups Turkey Potato Salad.

On your most elegant platter, shape the potato salad into an oval form, simulating the shape of the original breast carcass. Visualize how the breast would be positioned on each side of the carcass to recreate the original bird.

Carefully slice one (half) breast into *thin* slices, cutting diagonally across the grain, preserving the sequence of slices and the shape of the (half) breast. Then slice the other (half) breast in the same way but *creating a mirror image* with the slices.

Lay one breast, with its slices in sequence, on each side of the mounded salad, angling the slices to meet at the top in a chevron pattern.

Decorate with hard-cooked egg slices, tomatoes, green and black olives, capers, and greens. This striking presentation allows you to be as creative as you wish with your garnish.

Turkey Potato Salad

4 cups leftover cooked turkey, diced

3 cups red potatoes, freshly cooked, peeled, and diced

1-1/2 cups small peas, briefly cooked and cooled

1/2 cup green onions, including the tops, sliced

6 eggs, hard-cooked and grated

6 tablespoons minced sweet gherkins (optional)

3 tablespoons Dijon-style mustard

1/2 teaspoon celery seeds

Splash of tarragon vinegar

Salt

1-1/2 cups mayonnaise (or more as needed), preferably homemade

Parsley

Cherry tomatoes

Mix all the ingredients except the parsley and tomatoes lightly in a salad bowl, taking care to keep the mixture firm and not mushy. Garnish with parsley and cherry tomatoes.

Serves 8 to 10.

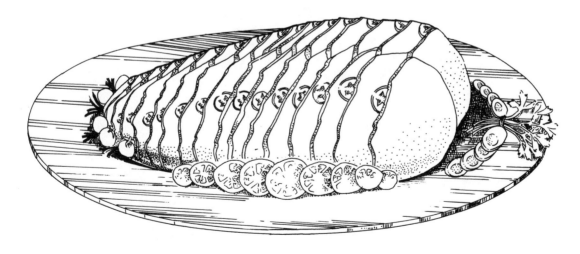

Olga Bier is a teacher-writer and home economist. She currently teaches catering and restaurant cookery for the Regional Occupational Program in Danville and is working on two food-related books (including a textbook on food service training). She is formerly a food writer for a number of newspapers, including having written the popular column, "Potluck with Olga Bier."

In addition to her interests in cooking, Ms. Bier has co-authored four musical plays and a one-act play which have been performed to critical acclaim.

Ms. Bier has two married daughters and lives in Martinez, California, with her husband, Harry.

Ken Wolfe is Instructor and Chair of the Culinary Arts Department at Contra Costa College, addresses audiences at special culinary events, and acts as a consultant in areas related to cuisine.

Chef Wolfe was born, educated, and trained in Vienna. From there he traveled to Shanghai, Hong Kong, Montreal, and finally to San Francisco. He served as executive chef or manager at restaurants in each of those cities.

For the past 20 years Chef Wolfe has been doing what he loves most: teaching and lecturing in the culinary arts. He won the prestigious Antonin Carême Medal; he was president of the Chefs' Association of the Pacific Coast twice; he is an elected member of the American Academy of Chefs and Epsilon Pi Tau honor society, and holds memberships in many other culinary organizations.

Chef Wolfe is the author of the much used and highly respected culinary textbook, *Cooking for the Professional Chef.*

Ken Wolfe has a grown daughter and lives in Lafayette, California, with his wife, Janet.

Maggie Blyth Klein is the author of *The Feast of the Olive* (Aris), a fine cook and editor, and will be opening her own restaurant in Berkeley in early 1985.

Charles Perry is a food historian and the restaurant critic for *California Magazine.* He frequently contributes to food magazines and is the author of *The Haight-Ashbury—A History* (Random House).

★ ★

Other Aris Books from Addison-Wesley

★ ★

THE ART OF FILO COOKBOOK by Marti Sousanis.   International entrees, appetizers, and desserts wrapped in flaky pastry. 144 pages, paper $10.95, ISBN 0-201-10871-2

FROM A BAKER'S KITCHEN by Gail Sher.   A comprehensive guide to the art of baking. 224 pages, paper $11.95, ISBN 0-201-11539-5

Available at your local bookstore. Or address orders or inquiries about these or other Addison-Wesley cookbooks to: Retail Sales Group, Addison-Wesley Publishing Company, Route 128, Reading, MA 01867. Order Department or Customer Service: 1-800-447-2226.